D0204932

生　存　汉　语

Survival Chinese

〔美〕唐·斯诺　编著

Don Snow

商　务　印　书　馆

The Commercial Press

2003·Beijing

图书在版编目(CIP)数据

生存汉语/(美)斯诺(Snow,Don)编著.—北京:商务印书馆,2002
ISBN 7-100-03166-4

Ⅰ.生…　Ⅱ.斯…　Ⅲ.对外汉语教学-教材
Ⅳ.H195.4

中国版本图书馆CIP数据核字(2000)第36496号

SHĒNGCÚN HÀNYǓ
生 存 汉 语
SURVIVAL CHINESE
〔美〕唐·斯诺　编著
Don Snow

商 务 印 书 馆 出 版
(北京王府井大街36号　邮政编码100710)
商 务 印 书 馆 发 行
北京中科印刷有限公司印刷
ISBN 7-100-03166-4/H·803

2002年1月第1版　　开本 787×960　1/32
2003年4月北京第2次印刷　　印张 10 3/4
定价:15.00元

Table of Contents

starters. Photos. Seeing guests off. Saying what someone does for a living. Signs: photo developing services.

Les 24 Personal Questions .... (299)

Responding to personal questions foreigners often hear in China. Age. Marital status.

Glossary .... (307)

Materials For Further Chinese Study .... (328)

Introduction: Why Another Beginning Chinese Textbook?

Many Chinese language textbooks are intended mainly for people who study Chinese in formal Chinese classes, and are based on assumptions that are appropriate primarily for such learners. The words and phrases such textbooks introduce in early lessons are often those that help students function in a classroom setting. Such texts also assume that learners' need to learn to read and write Chinese is as pressing as their need to speak it, so they introduce oral and written skills at the same rate. Underlying many such texts is also the assumption that they will be taught by a teacher, someone who will manage and guide the Chinese learning process for students.

However, what of people who will live or work in China but do not have the opportunity to study Chinese in a formal classroom setting? Such people usually need to become "street functional" in Chinese relatively quickly, so their most pressing need is for the words and phrases that will help them deal with daily life in China. Also, during their first weeks in China, such people often have a much greater need to learn to speak and understand basic Chinese than they have to learn Chinese characters. Finally, such learners usually need to take charge of their own language learning process, either studying with a tutor or studying on their own and then going out to practice with whatever Chinese people they encounter.

Survival Chinese is intended for this special category of Chinese learners, those people who are going to work or live in China for an extended period of time but who do not have the opportunity to study in a formal Chinese language program. It tries to meet the special needs of these learners in several ways:

1) It introduces "survival Chinese"—those words, phrases, sentence patterns and skills that are needed most often in daily life in China. The topics and content of lessons have been selected and organized so as to make learners functional on the street in China as quickly as

possible. Thus from the first day, rather than learning how to interact socially with classmates and talk about a classroom, students learn how to buy things, use the post office, get food in a restaurant, get assistance when something goes wrong, take buses and taxis, and so forth. Obviously only the most basic elements of Chinese are introduced here, and learners will need to move into other textbooks if they hope to progress beyond the minimal survival stage, but the language tools (vocabulary, phrases, and sentence patterns) presented here are sufficient to get learners through some of the most commonly encountered situations — and also to prepare them for further Chinese study.

2) *Survival Chinese* encourages learners to make their own choices as to where to focus their efforts; especially with regard to the question of how much time and attention to devote initially to learning to read and write Chinese. Some learners will initially want to ignore Chinese characters and focus all their attention on speaking and listening. Others will want to dabble a little in characters but still invest most of their time in oral skills. Yet others will want to work on both written and spoken skills right from the start. Thus each unit

has a core lesson for those interested mainly in oral skills, but also contains options for those who wish to begin characters. Material addressing Chinese tones, pronunciation, and *Pinyin* spelling (Romanization) is also presented in a separate section to serve either as an introduction or for review and reference.

3) *Survival Chinese* recognizes that learners may be studying individually with tutors or teachers who may have little experience teaching Chinese to foreigners (or whose ideas about teaching Chinese don't coincide with the learner's needs), and that an important part of Chinese study in such situations is learning how to work effectively with tutors who know Chinese but don't know how to teach it. In other words, learners need to learn how to gently turn well-meaning native speakers of Chinese into effective language teachers.

Underlying *Survival Chinese* there are several important assumptions:

1) SC assumes that learners have different needs, interests, and learning strategies, and it is thus designed to accommodate a variety of different approaches to Chinese, especially individual decisions as to how much attention learners initially wish to devote to Chinese

characters.

2)SC assumes that people learn any language by first mastering that which is simple and only gradually moving into that which is more complex, so in the initial stages of Chinese language study, it is less important that explanations be thorough than that they be clear and easy to understand. SC keeps explanations brief and relies heavily on examples to illustrate points of sentence construction and word order.

3)Finally, and most importantly, SC operates under the assumption that as a language learner you are most likely to succeed if you take charge of your own learning program. In practice this means that *you* need to choose the goals that are appropriate to your needs, *you* need to choose the study methods that fit your situation and learning style, *you* need to actively seek out and take advantage of opportunities to practice your Chinese, and *you* need to learn how to give direction to your teachers and tutors.

Acknowledgements

This material has developed over the past several years as part of an orientation program conducted for foreign language teachers newly arrived in China, and I owe a debt of gratitude to the teachers and staff of both the Amity Foundation and Nantong Teachers College. In particular, Tong Su and Cao Jingxin checked portions of early drafts for infelicities in the Chinese, and Huang Huixin and Hong Yuan made valuable editing suggestions based on their use of the material. Holly Herrin provided a Chinese menu that was useful in Lesson 13, and Joy Hilbun contributed the list of medicines available in China that is found in Lesson 18. Thanks to Ian Groves for a variety of contributions and suggestions, and to Caroline Fielder for interviewing a number of users of early drafts of this book. Many teachers working in China through the Amity Foundation and its partner groups have been gracious enough to provide feedback on early drafts of the book: Berit Aspegren, Georgina Baisley, Sandy and Christine Balfour, Helge Berge, Richard Brunt, Julie Chrystal, David Conkey, Sandy Cullers, Bill Davis, Julie Dennison, Ann Fishwick, Pamela Gordon, Stephen Graham, Melvena Green, Kay Grimmesey, Jean and Jostein Gronset, Hannah Henry, Lynne and Jon Hilton, Martin Johnson, Anne Kavanagh, Brit-Marie Lundback, Kay

Martin, Debbie Nicholson, Randi Nordby, Clayton Olson, Mary Carol Perrott, Julie Petrie, Kevin Plunkett, Fiona Pollard, Jonathan Robinson, Mirzah Rodriguez, Judy Scheckel, Mark Scott, Margareta Skov, Susan Smith, Esther Snader, Marit and Aril Sto, Eileen Summerville, Jane Thompson, Heina van Beijnum, Johanna and Landon van Dyke, Bill Voelker, Edith Warner, Robbie Wellington, Zandra Wells, Christina Wiklund, and Mike Williams. Thanks also to the many Nantong Teachers College students who have made suggestions as they used this material to tutor Amity teachers over the last few years. Last but not least my gratitude to Wei Hong Snow, who was always willing to provide emergency editorial services when I made last minute changes to the Chinese texts.

Studying Chinese With This Book

How Each Lesson Is Organized

Underlying each lesson in *Survival Chinese* is a set of daily life communication problems — such as how to buy a stamp or get something to eat at a noodle stand — of the kind that you will face from your very first day living in China. The goal of each lesson is to provide you with the basic language tools (vocabulary, phrases, sentence patterns, and strategies) that will enable you to cope with these daily life situations using rudimentary (but ever improving) Chinese.

Each lesson is divided into four basic parts:

Part 1: Core Lesson. This part of the lesson introduces the basic language tools — vocabulary, phrases, and sentence patterns — that you need in order to cope with whatever daily life situation the particular lesson deals with. This part of each lesson contains several sections:

Dialogue: Each Dialogue portrays a common daily life situation and the basic language tools and strategies you need for coping with the situation. The Dialogue is presented in both *Pinyin* (Romanization) and Chinese characters, and English translation is provided for each Chinese sentence. Eyebrows may be raised by the fact that the English translations are very literal — even to the point of being pidgin English. The danger in this is that the English translations may appear to caricature or even mock the Chinese. Please be assured that this is not at all my intent. I have used such literal translations because their word-by-word nature preserves Chinese sentence structure and wording as much as possible, and previous users have found that this helps them more quickly develop a feel for Chinese word order. (A more natural translation of the Dialogue appears at the end of each lesson.)

Dialogue Vocabulary: This is a listing of all new Chinese words that are used in the Dialogue, each with a simple gloss in English.

Additional Vocabulary: This is a listing of new

Chinese words that appear elsewhere in the lesson and additional words that are pertinent to the topic. As much as possible, words closely related to the same topic or situation are grouped together in one lesson so that they are easier to find and refer to. (Occasionally words are introduced in more than one lesson, mainly for the benefit of users who choose to use the lessons in an order different from the one in which they are presented in the book.)

Useful Phrases: This section presents short useful phrases relevant to the topic. Each phrase is followed by a literal English translation in parentheses; where necessary, a more natural English translation is also provided.

Sentence Patterns: Each lesson introduces one or more basic Chinese sentence patterns, each introduced by a question — such as "How do I state what time it is?"— stating the problem that the pattern will help you deal with. The patterns are introduced in this way under the assumption that they are best learned as tools for specific purposes rather than as arbitrary word combinations.

Part 2: Notes. This part of each lesson contains

comments on new words and points of usage which require elaboration. Here you will also find suggested strategies for dealing with daily life situations, and tips on language learning.

Part 3: Practice Ideas. When studying Chinese with tutors or on your own, you may sometimes run out of ideas for what to do with your study or practice time. The Practice Ideas part of each lesson is a list of suggested practice activities, relevant to the topic, which you can do with your tutor or on your own. (A general list of practice activities that can be used for all lessons can be found in "Working With Tutors.") Past users of this material have tended to draw on these suggestions sparingly and selectively, but have found it helpful to have them available for times when creative juices run a bit dry.

Part 4: Extra Credit. This final part of each lesson contains things which will probably only be of interest to some learners. It generally consists of two sections:

Survival Characters: This section selectively introduces the characters that should prove most useful to you in the early stages of finding your way around China. Included are common characters found on signs, maps, menus, etc.

Extra Credit Vocabulary: For topics where it is helpful to have longer lists of new words than you could reasonably be expected to study and remember (for example, lists of foods) this is the part of the lesson where such lists are included. These can be used for study or reference.

Using Survival Chinese

The intent of this book is most definitely *not* that you work through it from beginning to end, studying all the material and doing all the exercises. Think of this book more as a menu of language material and learning methods from which you choose whatever suits your purposes. As much as possible, the material in this book has been designed and organized in such a way that it is flexible and user-friendly, allowing you to carry out a Chinese study program that suits your own needs and interests.

There is no end to the variety of different ways in which you could use the material in this book, but to help you get started thinking let me suggest a few basic plans:

Plan A: The First-Month-in-China Spoken Chinese Plan. What many people want and need during their first weeks in China is survival speaking and listening skills. Focusing your efforts on speaking and listening enables you to quickly learn how to get around China and meet your survival needs. This approach to the first stages of Chinese study also generates a lot of positive reinforcement because daily you can use what you learn and see your skills improve; also, as you speak to Chinese people you will generally find that they are generous with praise and encouragement for foreigners who make the effort to try to learn their language. Even if you eventually hope to learn to read and write Chinese, it might make sense to narrow your efforts to speaking and listening for a few weeks until you feel comfortable dealing with the most common daily situations.

If this sounds like the plan for you, a good strategy for using this book might be to:

1) Study the Core Lesson in each lesson, learning basic words and sentence patterns. As you study the first few lessons, you may also want to look at the sections of this book that introduce Chinese *Pinyin*

spelling, pronunciation, and tones.

2) Ignore the Chinese characters in the lessons, and also any of the Extra Credit material that is not immediately useful to you.

3) Devote a lot of time to speaking and listening practice, both in and out of class. The Practice Ideas section may be useful in helping you find productive ways to practice with your tutor or other Chinese people.

Plan B: The Speaking + Survival Reading Plan. Some people want to begin studying selected Chinese characters right from the beginning of their study program, but do not want to slow down their progress in speaking and listening by investing the time it would take to learn the Chinese character for each new word they learn. Even during your first weeks in China it can be very useful to learn the most common Chinese characters found on street signs, maps, menus, and so forth in your environment. While it may be some time before you know enough characters to read all of a sign, even being able to read one or two of the characters often provides you with enough clues to determine whether or not this is the right bus, the school you are looking for, the proper bathroom door, or whatever. The other advantage of studying some Chinese characters right from the start is that as you learn to recognize a few characters they will soon come to seem less intimidating and foreign to you; in fact, many people come to be fascinated by Chinese characters and find that learning how to read and write them becomes one of the most appealing aspects of learning Chinese.

If this plan sounds good, a suggested approach would be:

1) Follow Plan A above for speaking and listening skills.

2) Also study the Survival Characters in each lesson. At first you may only want to learn to recognize them, but you could also have your tutor point out the radicals from which most characters are constructed (this will help you remember them) and perhaps show you how to write them.

3) When walking on the streets, get into the habit of looking at signs and so forth for Chinese characters that you know. This effort is not only a good way to review and memorize the characters you study in the book, but also gets you in the habit of paying attention

and trying to make sense of the written Chinese in your environment. (Otherwise, you will probably get into the habit of simply ignoring it.) You might even carry a little notebook with you for jotting down new characters that look interesting to you or appear frequently enough to be worth learning.

Plan C: The Total Mastery Plan. If you are sure that your eventual goal is mastery of both written and spoken Chinese, you might choose to invest significant effort in developing oral and written skills right from the beginning. Making a broad frontal attack on Chinese requires a fair investment of time if you are to progress at a rate that makes you feel satisfied; for Westerners it takes longer to learn Chinese than it does many other foreign languages, mainly because of the investment of time required to learn to read and write. However, the benefit of this plan is that it will give you a good foundation for future efforts to learn to read, write and speak Chinese.

1) If this is what you need, one suggested approach would be to study all or most of material in each lesson. In particular, learn to read and write the Chinese characters in the Core Dialogues instead of just learning

how to say them.

2) An alternative would be to quickly skim through this book to get your survival skills, following one of the two plans above, before starting to study with another text series that devotes fuller attention to reading. This would give you a jump-start in your Chinese study, getting you out practicing on the streets sooner than most text series and programs would. (Many text series and programs have the unintended effect of encouraging you to keep your head in the textbook too long before getting out to use what you learn.)

Clearly, no one of these plans is the "right" plan in any universal sense, and there are endless variations on each. The right plan for you is the one which provides the best match between your goals, your learning style, and the amount of time and effort you are willing to invest. Also, none of these plans is ever set in stone, and as you move along in your Chinese study you will no doubt want to set new goals and experiment with new approaches as you not only gain greater command of Chinese but also a better knowledge of what approaches to language learning work best for you.

Making a plan for your study of Chinese

As you go about making your plan for Chinese study, you need to be realistic about the fact that independent language study also poses some special problems, and a plan of Chinese study which doesn't take these problems into account has a relatively low chance of success. Here are a few of the issues you need to consider:

1) **Limits on your time and energy**: Presumably most foreigners who can study Chinese full-time will be in formal language programs (both for academic and visa reasons), so those who take an independent study approach are often in China for work-related reasons and generally have job, family or other obligations which make it impossible to study Chinese full time. This means that finding time in your schedule for Chinese lessons, study, and practice may be difficult, and your other obligations (which generally seem more immediately pressing) may encroach on — and even overwhelm — your Chinese study. Even if you have enough time in your schedule for a regular but limited study program, you will need to be on guard against

discouragement because your progress under such circumstances may only be gradual.

2) **Absence of outside pressure**: One of the great advantages of formal language programs is that tests, grades, and the watching eye of the teacher provide constant (if rather artificial) pressure to keep studying. Students in formal programs are often essentially forced to keep studying, and when their will fails there are outside prods to ensure that their efforts don't flag. In contrast, as an independent learner you will usually be under little or no outside pressure to keep studying Chinese. There are usually no tests to worry about, and a tutor you have personally hired (and can dismiss at any time) is much less likely to pressure you than a teacher in a formal program. Also, foreigners who don't speak Chinese can generally get by in China using English (though the results often aren't very pretty), so pressure from the environment is actually much weaker than one might initially imagine. All of this means that you will probably be tempted from time to time by the knowledge that you can choose to put off studying Chinese — or even to give it up completely — more or less at will. Much is therefore demanded of your will

power and self-discipline, more than is the case for students in formal programs.

3) **Absence of structure**: While the goals and methods of a formal language program may not fully match the needs of a given learner, a structured program spares that learner the effort of creating a study program from scratch, and also provides the learner with a sense of direction and progress through the program. In contrast, as an independent learner, more is demanded of you because you need to design your own program. At the practical level, this means going through the effort of setting your own goals, choosing your own study materials and methods, finding a tutor, and finding ways to evaluate and measure your own progress. At the affective level, you may also be less certain about whether or not your approach to Chinese study is "right," especially if you have limited previous experience with language learning, and this sense of uncertainty may subtly corrode your confidence and resolution. This is especially likely if you adopt a very informal approach to Chinese study, doing a little of this and a little of that without much continuity or sense of plan. Relatively unorganized study approaches often

leave learners feeling that they aren't learning much (either because they genuinely aren't or because the absence of structure in their approach denies them bench posts against which they can measure — and see — their progress), and this sets the stage for deciding that Chinese study isn't worth the effort.

As you have probably noticed, the underlying theme in the problems discussed above is not so much one of technique as it is of feelings, and this suggests one of the most basic truths of language learning: The key to success in language learning is generally sustained effort more than a special technique or a "gift for languages," so the most important issue is whether or not you can sustain the learning effort over a period of time. The main problem faced by most independent language learners is that is relatively easy for them to opt out of the Chinese learning process if they become discouraged or feel they are not making enough progress to justify the effort. Designing a good study plan is thus to a large degree a question of how to carry out a program of study that you won't give up on. With this problem in mind, here are a few suggestions you may wish to consider as you begin setting out your Chinese study program:

1) ***Be realistic about your time and energy*:**

The first step to successfully sustaining a program of Chinese study is realistically assessing how much time and energy you have to devote to the task, and then designing a study approach that fits within the time you have available. A common mistake learners make, especially when just starting out on Chinese study (and still filled with energy) is making an overly optimistic assessment of their time and energy, and then setting goals that are far too high. The problem here is that when learners begin running out of steam, and especially if they fall far below the goals they set, they often get discouraged and quit, either putting off Chinese study until they have more time (a situation which often never materializes) or simply abandoning the effort altogether.

The first step to realistic planning is making a good assessment of how much time a day you can devote to Chinese study, and also being realistic about how much energy you will have at those times of day when you are free to study. (Obviously, you can't expect to learn as much in an hour of Chinese study at a time of day when you are exhausted as you could in an hour when you are more fresh and alert.) Learners who stick with it will continue to make progress, and even slow-but-steady study efforts can deliver impressive results if sustained.

2) ***Setting limited goals and focusing your efforts*:**

As suggested above, overly ambitious goals often actually undermine learners' morale, so it is important that you set reasonably limited goals that you can realistically achieve with the time and energy you have available. One implication of this idea is that it is often wise to focus on a relatively narrow set of goals, especially during the early stages of Chinese learning. For example, it may make more sense for busy people to focus their initial efforts on speaking and listening, only turning later to Chinese characters. The difficulty with trying to make a full-scale assault on Chinese, working on speaking, listening, reading, and writing simultaneously, is that dividing limited time among so many goals will probably result in slow progress toward each, and this tends to be discouraging. In contrast, a narrower focus allows you to make more visible progress in the skills of areas you focus on, and encourages you to keep going.

3) ***Rewards***:

Independent Chinese study places more demands on your self-discipline than formal Chinese classes do. As noted above, even if you work with a tutor there will still be less outside pressure placed on you than would be the case in formal Chinese classes, and there may also be periods of time when you can't find a tutor you work with comfortably — and when you therefore don't have a tutor to drive on your study efforts. Thus, you need to supply the discipline for your own learning process if you don't want the whole thing to dissolve into a puddle of good intentions.

When it comes to persuading yourself to study Chinese at the crack of dawn or after a long day at work, you are more likely to actually study if you are doing something you find enjoyable, rewarding, or at least useful. Thus, someone who loves to chat will probably have more motivation for sessions with a tutor, or perhaps for learning some new phrases to try out on the local store clerk, while someone who is fascinated by

Chinese characters may be willing to sit down and draw characters with a brush when he/she wouldn't have enough motivation to listen to tapes. Know yourself, and as much as possible design your study approach so that your interests pull you along.

4) ***Structure*:**

Some people learn fairly well just doing whatever they feel like doing on any given day, but for most people a casual irregular approach to language learning is a recipe for failure. Perhaps the greatest problem with unstructured approaches to language learning is that they lack the visible indications of achievement that are present in more structured approaches, and learners who don't have the advantage of the encouragement provided by these measures of achievement are more prone to a sense that they aren't making progress.

There are a variety of ways structure can be introduced into independent Chinese study. One of the most obvious is through use of a textbook or other Chinese study materials — your progress through the materials provides a visible sense of satisfaction and accomplishment. Another is through setting and adhering to a regular schedule of study and practice. In this case, the amount of your time investment becomes a measure of achievement. A third, less obvious, approach involves establishing a cycle of activities that you carry out for each lesson in your book or topic that you study. For example, a cycle might consist of: Step #1: Studying a certain lesson in your book. Step #2: Practicing material from the lesson with a tutor. Step #3: Trying the new material out in the community, for example, by chatting with the clerk at the local store. Step #4: At the next lesson, asking your tutor about anything puzzling that occurred in your real life practice. In this approach, achievement is measured in the number of cycles you carry out. (One advantage of this approach is that it not only provides structure for your program, but also includes a healthy dose of live practice.)

5) ***Find a support group*:**

To a degree that might be surprising, your ability to sustain study of Chinese will be affected by the company you keep. Unlike learners in formal Chinese programs, who have a ready-made support group of fellow learners, many of the people you live and work with — especially other Westerners — may not share your interest in learning Chinese. If this is the case, you will probably get only minimal encouragement in your Chinese learning efforts, and you may well face at least some social pressure not to devote too much time to Chinese. (Keep in mind that many Westerners in China explain their failure to learn Chinese by arguing that it is simply too hard, and your progress in Chinese may make others look bad by comparison.) It is thus important that you try to find at least one or two people — either other Westerners or Chinese — who will support and encourage you as you learn Chinese.

6) ***Making your own plan*:**

The strategy assumed by all of the suggestions above is that you need to take charge of your own Chinese language learning by investing time in making your own plan for Chinese study. Among the issues which you will need to consider are:

— What are your initial study goals? For example, do you wish initially to focus on speaking and listening skills, or do you want to work on Chinese characters right from the start?

— What study materials will you use? For example, if you are working with a textbook, you might consider also having your tutor make language tapes for you to increase your amount of listening practice. If so, what kind of material would be best to put on the tape?

— How are you going to spend your study time? Again, assuming you are working with some kind of textbook, what is the best way for you to learn the material in any given lesson? (Keep in mind that different people often have very different learning styles, so through trial and error you need to find approaches that work well for you.)

— How do you wish to spend any time you have with a tutor? (See further discussion of this question in "Working with Tutors.")

— How will you practice the material you learn outside language class? You need to practice if you are to really master the material you study, so it is important to find ways to practice your Chinese in the community.

Obviously it takes some time and effort to think about all of these things, and this list of questions may have left you longing for a teacher who would simply tell you what to do. But by deciding these issues for yourself you take advantage of the opportunity to tailor-make your own approach to Chinese study, an approach that suits your own goals, personality, learning style and skill levels much better than any off-the-rack Chinese class could. Learners who take control of their Chinese learning this way generally wind up with a study program that gives them a high level of return for the effort they invest, and this provides excellent conditions for significant progress in learning Chinese.

Working With Tutors

It is not absolutely necessary to work with tutors in order to carry out an independent Chinese study program; some learners make considerable progress by studying on their own and taking advantage of whatever practice opportunities come their way. However, most people who try to learn Chinese without the benefit of regular classes find it helpful to have more-or-less regular contact with a tutor or at least with a friend who will assist them with Chinese. Working with a tutor provides you with extensive practice opportunities in a relatively safe environment, allowing you to try out and rehearse new language skills with a friendly mentor before going out into the (sometimes less merciful) street. Regular contact with a tutor also helps provide structure and accountability to your language study.

What should you look for in a tutor?

When a foreigner starts looking for a Chinese teacher, it is often assumed that the ideal candidate needs a perfect Beijing accent, extensive experience in language teaching, and a good command of English. Needless to say, it is not always easy to find such a person. More to the point, such people don't necessarily make good tutors. Of course, if they really know what they are doing, the experience of such people will be a real advantage, but it can also be a problem because language teachers tend to have rather fixed notions about language teaching and may not be very open to your suggestions. (Some language teachers in China — either teachers of Chinese or English — are accustomed to a teacher-centered approach in which the teacher makes all the decisions and students are relatively passive.)

So, what should you be looking for in a tutor? A few suggestions:

1) The most important thing is finding someone who is comfortable to work with, encouraging, enjoyable to be with, but who still helps you learn Chinese. This is

probably more important in the long run than other factors like accent and teaching experience.

2) It is also important to find someone who will cooperate with you in the carrying out of *your* plan. To this end, it is sometimes better to work with people who are somewhat younger than you (less likely to pull rank), or non-professionals (less likely to have strong notions about what you should do), or people who are by personality easy to work with.

3) Accent: It is good for your tutor to have a reasonably standard accent, or at least to be able to approximate one when speaking to you, but don't let a moderate local accent put you off from working with someone who you are otherwise comfortable with.

4) Language teaching experience: This is good if it doesn't result in your tutor having an overwhelming desire to control, but experience is probably less important than willingness to spend time practicing with you and to cooperate in the carrying out of your plan.

5) Ability to speak English/your native language: If you feel a strong need to have things explained to you, then it is important to have a tutor who speaks your language. However, do not automatically assume that

this is essential. Many of the Chinese textbooks available in China provide explanation in English, and frequently it is better for you to experiment and figure things out on your own anyway. Also, if you insist that your tutor have good English, you cut down drastically on the number of acceptable candidates. What you need in a tutor is a willing practice partner more than a living grammar book, and a good practice partner need not be able to explain everything to you (though some people have a knack for keeping things simple and clear, and this is a real asset in a tutor). I would encourage you to consider not limiting your tutor search to those who speak English, or at least not to those who speak English well.

Finding a tutor

It can be difficult to find a good Chinese tutor, so be prepared to invest some time and effort in the search. You may well go through several tutors who are less than ideal before eventually finding someone who you can work with comfortably, so try not to be discouraged if the process takes a while. There is much to be said for being slow and careful about picking your first tutor;

once you have a tutor it is generally awkward and difficult to break off and find a new one.

Some tips on locating tutors:

1) You will probably start your search by asking for help from Chinese people you know, perhaps someone where you work or live, and this approach often produces candidates fairly quickly. However, once a person is recommended it can be awkward for you to refuse, and you may wind up with someone who is not ideal. One way to cope with this problem is to tell your potential matchmaker in advance that you are looking for someone to help you for a specified period of time (three months, one semester, etc.). You might also say that over time you will want to have different tutors so that you can get used to different accents. This gives you a natural excuse for bowing out if things don't go well.

2) If you ask for help locating a tutor, people may assume you need someone with a Beijing accent, a grounding in Chinese literature, or whatever, so be sure to invest the time necessary to explain to matchmakers what *you* want in a tutor.

3) Be prepared for the possibility that the person you ask to match-make may well volunteer him/herself.

It can be very awkward to refuse, so if you are worried about a person volunteering, don't tell him/her you want a tutor. On the other hand, asking someone to help you search can be a good indirect way to see if that person might be interested in tutoring you.

4) If you are a teacher, having one of your own students tutor you may not be such a good idea — too much potential for role confusion or the appearance of favoritism. It is often better to have a student from someone else's class, or perhaps a student from an informal class where grades and favoritism aren't issues.

5) It may be a good idea to choose a tutor who is slightly outside your immediate community. This gives you access to another circle of people, and also makes it easier to end the tutoring relationship if necessary without creating too much ill will among people you see every day.

The question of pay

One headache in working with tutors in China is figuring out how to compensate them. Many tutors will say you don't need to give them anything, but accepting such generosity can be problematic because it places you in a position of obligation where you have little control over how your debt will be repaid. Some people would never take advantage of you, but others might later make uncomfortable requests that would be hard to refuse. Some ways to cope with the compensation problem:

1) Pay: Some tutors in China will accept pay with little or no hesitation. For those who will accept pay, this compensation method has the advantage of keeping roles and responsibilities clear and preventing obligation build-up. (Before deciding how much to pay your tutor, try to get a sense of the local going rate for tutoring. There is nothing wrong with your being generous within the normal pay range for such services, but if the pay you offer is way off the scale, others in the community may resent the sweet deal your tutor is getting.)

However, many potential tutors in China will be reluctant to accept financial compensation because they feel exchange of money would make the relationship seem too cold and mercenary. Some of these might eventually be willing to accept pay if it is given to them in a very low key manner or through a third party. For others, it may be necessary to find another approach to compensation.

2) Language exchanges: One common solution to the compensation problem is a language exchange in which you offer tutoring in English or another language in exchange for tutoring in Chinese. This approach has the advantage of keeping money out of the equation, hence making the whole set-up seem friendlier, yet still preventing you from being placed in a position of too much obligation. The disadvantage of this solution is that it cuts into your precious time. Also, unless there are clear guidelines as to who is practicing which language when, you may find that you are teaching English more than learning Chinese (especially as it is likely that your tutor's English will be better than your Chinese, hence making it easier to chat in English).

3) Other kinds of exchanges: You may be able to exchange lessons of some other kind (cooking, guitar, etc.) for tutoring in Chinese.

4) Gifts: If tutors won't accept money directly, you might repay them with occasional meals or nice presents.

Working with a tutor

It may be some time before you and your tutor are on the same wavelength. Initially your tutor may assume that it is his/her job to "teach" you Chinese, i.e. to explain everything to you, prepare lessons, etc. Your tutor may also start out with notions of what you need to learn and how you should learn it that are quite different from yours. So, be prepared to tactfully and patiently help your tutors think of themselves more as informants who assist you in your study efforts than as teachers who plan and direct your study efforts. A good way to start is by stating your desires very clearly to whoever helps you locate tutors, and to the tutors themselves when you first meet to discuss your plans. Even if your tutors do not fully understand at first, by raising the issue you have forewarned them that they should not simply operate under whatever assumptions they already have about teaching you.

You will find it easier to maintain control of your study program if you are the one who plans how the time in your tutoring sessions will be used. If you go into a tutorial with a plan or at least a short list of ideas, your tutor will be less tempted to set a different agenda. Of course this takes more effort on your part, but it also results in much better use of your tutorial time and in your learning more Chinese.

Activity ideas for study time with tutors

An hour spent working one-on-one with a tutor generally allows you far more practice and learning opportunity than an hour spent sitting in a larger language class, but it also generally requires more preparation on your part. One reason you need to prepare more is that responsibility for how the hour is spent lies with you more than with the tutor, and if you don't have a plan of action, it is easy for useful activity to grind to a halt — and for the lesson to turn into a chatting session (often in English).

A second reason you need to invest time in planning your tutorial sessions is that an hour spent working one-on-one with a tutor is generally much more mentally and emotionally intense and demanding than an hour spent sitting in class. In a larger class, it is rare for any one student to be "on stage" for more than a small fraction of the class period. During much of the class period most students are engaged in activities of a lower pressure nature, listening to other students interact with the teacher, talking in small groups, reading, and so forth. However, during a one-to-one tutorial you are on stage constantly, and there are fewer natural breathing spaces in the lesson. Because of this it is important that the lesson plan contain a variety of activities that prevents you from being overwhelmed by too much of any one activity. Also, the concentrated nature of tutorial lessons means that any given activity will probably run its natural course after a relatively short period of time, and it is therefore usually necessary to plan a greater number of activities in order to fill the hour. (This is especially true when your command of Chinese is insufficient to allow you to take up slack time by chatting with your tutor in Chinese.)

Each lesson in this book provides a short list of activity suggestions specific to the material in that lesson. However, in order to avoid repeating every suggestion in each lesson, activity ideas of a more general nature are listed here:

Review: It is often a good idea to start a lesson by repeating an activity from a previous lesson. Such review allows you to consolidate control of material, and also serves as a good warm-up before a new lesson.

Pronunciation practice, using the Dialogue: Many learners find it helpful to read the Dialogue aloud while the tutor assists with pronunciation and/or tones. This activity also helps you learn/review the material in the Dialogue, and provides a good opportunity to raise questions about any points in the Dialogue that are unclear.

Role-plays: A good way to consolidate material learned in the Dialogue is to role play the same situation with your tutor. You may find it helpful to do this more than once, switching roles with your tutor. This is generally more fun if you also improvise and expand on the original situation. Role playing is an excellent way for you to build both speaking and listening skills.

Tone/Pinyin dictation for new vocabulary: For each lesson you can expand on the vocabulary provided by asking your tutor to dictate additional vocabulary to you in Chinese while you write it down in *Pinyin*. (You can indicate what words you want to know by pointing to objects, showing pictures, giving the English equivalents, or whatever.) This activity not only helps you learn new words, but also builds your ability to hear sounds and tones, and to write down words in *Pinyin* for your notebook.

Presumably your tutor should check your *Pinyin* transcriptions, but many Chinese do not have a very strong command of *Pinyin*, so you may need to check some words in a dictionary. Keep in mind that your tutor's pronunciation may well not be entirely standard — only a small percentage of the Chinese population speaks a more or less standard form of Putonghua as their mother tongue — so over time you should learn what the peculiarities of the local accent are and learn to adjust for those as you transcribe into standard Putonghua.

Making sentences with new vocabulary and sentence patterns: One effective way to consolidate your command of new words and patterns is by trying to use them to make sentences. This is a good activity for time spent with your tutor because the tutor can give you feedback as to how correct and/or appropriate your attempts at sentence construction are. This is especially useful for gaining control of words and patterns whose usage is more problematic.

Translation practice: To check and build your command of Chinese vocabulary, phrases, and/or sentences, have your tutor say a word (phrase, sentence) in English and then you translate it into Chinese (or vice versa). This activity is good for checking whether or not you have learned material, and it also builds your ability to translate, a useful skill in and of itself.

Listening practice: One way to build your listening skills is to have your tutor tell you simple stories (dialogues, etc.) that are not too far above your listening comprehension range. The tutor then tells you the story one or more times, and follows up by asking you comprehension questions.

Initially almost any story in Chinese may be too hard for you to understand, so one approach you might try is to have the tutor base stories rather closely on Dialogues you have studied, using much of the same vocabulary but varying the plot line and perhaps adding a little new vocabulary. (This may seem a simple enough activity, but your tutor may still find this easier to do if given advance warning and time to prepare.)

Map, sign reading: To build survival reading

skills, study the Survival Characters in each lesson, and then look for these characters on Chinese maps, signs, and menus. (Flash cards may be helpful in learning these characters, not least because you can carry them around and practice with them when you have odd moments of free time.)

Dialogue reading: For those who choose to work on reading Chinese, one useful activity is having your tutor write out simple dialogues in Chinese characters for you to read, using words and structures from Dialogues you have studied.

Character writing: For those who choose to begin working on Chinese writing skills, you may want to make a habit of having your tutor show you the proper stroke order for writing Chinese characters from the lessons.

Chinese character dictation: To further develop your character writing skills, have your tutor dictate Chinese sentences, using words (characters) you have already studied, for you to write down in characters. This activity is a good way to provide accountability for your study of Chinese characters at beginning levels.

Taping: To enable you to practice listening at

home, ask your tutor to tape the Dialogue and other parts of the lesson for you. Listening to tapes is a good way to study and review, and by custom-making them in cooperation with your tutor you can design tapes so they are most effective for you. Learning to make language learning tapes that suit your learning needs and style is in and of itself an important skill for language learners to master.

Obviously it is more efficient time-wise for you if tutors make tapes for you on their own time rather than during the lesson. However, if you have your tutor make tapes during the lesson, you are present to let your tutor know if he/she is speaking too quickly or slowly. Also, taking a break in the middle of a tutoring session to make tapes allows you a (possibly much needed) breathing spell.

Chinese Pronunciation, *Pinyin*, and Tones

I. *Chinese Pronunciation and Pinyin* (*Romanized spelling*)

Westerners first learning Chinese often have the impression that it is very foreign and exotic sounding, therefore presumably difficult to pronounce. Actually, however, most of the sounds used in Chinese are similar to sounds used in English and other Western languages, and most of those sounds which are not familiar are not very difficult to learn. There are, of course, a few exceptions to this generalization, but not many. (The main reason Chinese sounds so different and foreign to Western ears has to do with tones, a problem we will address below.)

Chinese language books and study programs often begin with a rather long and detailed set of pronunciation exercises. Some learners find this to be a useful way to establish a foundation for later Chinese study; others find this phase of the learning process boring and not terribly useful. In the short introduction to Chinese *Pinyin* (Romanization) and pronunciation below, I assume my task is primarily to get you started out, so the introduction below strives less for thoroughness than brevity and clarity. I have said little about sounds that are very easy or similar to English, saving effort for more challenging sounds. Ultimately, however, the best way for you to learn pronunciation is to listen to and mimic your tutor and other Chinese people. Deciding how much pronunciation drill you need is up to you.

Chinese is a syllabic language, each word consisting of one or more short syllables. Traditionally Chinese consider each syllable as consisting of two parts, the initial and the final, and for the sake of convenience the introduction below will make use of this handy division.

Initials: A Listing

b- Like "b-" in "boy."

p- Like "p-" in "pie."

m- Like "m-" in "my."

f- Like "f-" in "for."

d- Like "d-" in "do."

t- Like "t-" in "to."

n- Like "n-" in "no."

l- Like "l-" in "like."

g- Like "g-" in "go."

k- Like "k-" in "key."

h- Like "h-" in "high", but a little more guttural.

y- Like "y-" in "you."

w- Like "w-" in "we."

s- Like "s-" in "so."

c- A "ts" sound, pronounced like the end of "cats."

z- A "dz" sound, pronounced like the end of "lids."

j- Like "j" in "jeep", but with the tongue just a little further forward.

q- Like "ch" in "cheap", but with the tongue just a little further forward.

x- Like "sh" in "she", but with the tongue just a little further forward.

zh- Like "j" in "jump", but with tip of the tongue a

little further back.

ch- Like "ch" in "chip", but with tongue further back.

sh- Like "sh" in "ship", but with tongue further back.

r- Like "r" in "rink", but with the tongue a bit higher so it buzzes ever so slightly.

Finals: A Listing

-a Like "a" as in "father" (American pronunciation).

-ai Like the "-y" in "sky."

-ao Like "ow" in "how."

-an Like "-an" in "Juan."

-ang Like "a" (as in "father") + -ng.

-e Like "uh" in English, similar to the "u" in "under."

-ei Like "-ay" as in "day."

-en Like "un" in "under", but with the vowel a little higher and further forward.

-eng Like "-ung" as in "hung."

-i Usually pronounced as "ee" as in "he."

But after c/s/z and ch/sh/zh/r it is pronounced as a short vowel, similar to "i" in "it."

-ia Like "ya" (a Swedish "yes").

-ie Sounds like the "ye" in "yet."

-iu Like "yo."

-iao Like "yow."

-in About halfway between "-een" as in "green" and "-in" as in "pin."

-ing Like English "ing", but the first sound a little higher and longer.

-ian Like "yen."

-iang Like "yang", rhyming with "-ang" above.

-iong Like "ong" (below), but preceded by a "y."

-o Like "wo." Lips do not close as the sound is made; instead they *open further*.

-ou Like "o" as in "go" (American pronunciation), lips closing slightly at end of sound.

-ong "ou" + "ng." No corresponding sound in English, but not difficult to make.

-u Usually pronounced "oo" as in "you."

But after j/q/x and sometimes n/l it is pronounced as an umlaut "u" (ü).

-ua Like "wa" as in "water."

-ui Like "way."

-uo Like "woe."

-uai Like the "wi-" in "wild", or like the word "why" (with no "h").

-uan Usually like "uan" in "Juan."

But if preceded by y/j/q/x this is pronounced like "-en" in "when."

-uang Like "wang," rhyming with "-ang" above.

-ü Like the umlaut "u" in German and French, a combination of "eee" and "ooo". (Make an "eee" sound with your jaw, and then round your lips for an "ooo" without moving your jaw.)

-ue "-ü" + "e" as in "wet."

-un "-ü" + "n."

Other syllables

er Similar to "er" in American English, but the mouth opened a little more.

wu Sounds like "woo."

yi Sounds like "yee."

yu "y" + "-ü."

Potential trouble spots

As noted above, most of the *Pinyin* Romanization system does not pose serious obstacles to speakers of English. There are, however, a few points that deserve a bit of extra attention.

1) **The retroflex sounds**: zh-, ch-, sh-, and r-. These initials are called "retroflex" sounds because they are all pronounced with the tongue curved back into the middle of mouth. For the first three of these, there is a corresponding sound that is pronounced further forward in the mouth, and one key to mastering standard Chinese pronunciation is being able to distinguish between the retroflex initial and its more forward counterpart. (More on this in a minute.) The pairs are:

1) zh- and j-. Both sound something like the "j" in "jump," but for zh- the tip of the tongue is a little further back and for j- it is further forward.

2) ch- and q-. Both are like the "ch" in "chip," but

for ch- the tongue is further back and for q- it is further forward.

3) sh- and x-. Both are like the "sh" in "ship," but for sh- the tongue is further back and for x- it is further forward.

Two important notes:

1) One way the sounds above are distinguished from each other is by the position of the tongue. However, they are also distinguished as much or more by the fact that j-, q-, and x- are always followed by a high front vowel, either -i (an "ee" sound) or -ü, and zh-, ch-, and sh- never are. So, even if you pronounce both members of a pair the same way there is little possibility of confusion as long as you get the rest of the word right.

2) Retroflex sounds are more typical of northern Chinese speech than that of other parts of China; in fact, in many parts of China people pronounce all these sounds with their tongue forward. Zh- thus becomes z-, ch- becomes c-, and sh- becomes s-. While you should try to pronounce them in a standard manner, your ears need to get used to the many Chinese speakers who don't make these distinctions. You may also take

comfort in the fact that many Chinese find the distinction between these pairs as troublesome as you may.

2) **Hard sounds**: In addition to the retroflex sounds discussed above, there are a few other sounds in Chinese that are just plain difficult for English-speaking Westerners to make.

r- Chief among the trouble makers is the initial retroflex sound r-. It is pronounced like the "r" in "rink", but with the tongue just a bit higher so that it buzzes ever so slightly. (Again, in many parts of China even Chinese people don't make this sound in a way that would pass for standard in Beijing, so you will be allowed some latitude in getting this one right.)

c- This "ts" sound does exist in English, but never at the beginnings of words. To make it, first say "cats" and then eliminate the "ca-" part.

-ü English does not have this sound (although German and French do). The simplest explanation is that this is a combination of "ooo" and "eee." To make it, make an "eee" sound with your jaw, and then round your lips for an "ooo" without moving your jaw.

3) **Tricky spellings**: On the whole the *Pinyin* system is quite logical — far more consistent than English spelling, for example — but there are a few anomalies that may trip you up if you are not careful.

-i Usually this is pronounced as "ee" as in "he."
But after the c-/s-/z- and ch-/sh-/zh-/r- sets it is pronounced as a short vowel, similar to the "i" in "it" and "in." The easiest way to cope with this is just to memorize that the following spellings require the short sound: ci, si, zi and chi, shi, zhi, ri.

-u Usually it is pronounced "oo" as in "you."
But after y-/j-/q-/x- it is pronounced as an umlaut "u" (ü). Again, the best thing to do is memorize that the following sounds require a "ü" sound: yu, ju, qu, xu, yun, jun, qun, xun.

To thicken the broth further, after n- and l-, -u is sometimes "u" (oo) and sometimes "ü." (Actually in this situation if the sound is the umlaut "ü," it should be marked as such, but usually Chinese know from context how it should be pronounced so the umlaut marking is sometimes omitted when the word is spelled out in *Pinyin*.)

-e When alone this is pronounced like "uh" in English, similar to the "u" in "under." But in the following combinations it is pronounced as follows:

-ie Sounds like the "ye" in "yet."

-ue Like the "we-" in "wet."

ye Again, like the "ye" in "yet."

-ian Despite the "a," this sound is pronounced like the word "yen." The same is true for:

yan Pronounced "yen."

-ui This is pronounced "way." (We might have expected this sound to be spelled *-uei, but no such luck. At least it isn't spelled "weigh.")

II. *Tones*

What are "tones"?

In Chinese, the intonation of a word is an integral part of its pronunciation. Thus a syllable pronounced with a high level intonation is a different word from the same syllable pronounced with a rising intonation, a falling-rising intonation, or a falling intonation. The classic example used to intimidate beginning learners of Chinese is the syllable ma, which means "mother" if pronounced with a high level intonation and "horse" if pronounced with a falling-rising intonation.

Westerners sometimes feel that they cannot hear tones, but this is not exactly what the problem is. After all, speakers of English listen to and use intonation all the time. Consider the difference between a rising tone "Yes?" (as someone answers the door) or a falling tone "Yes!" (as an enthusiastic response to an offer of free money). The difference between Chinese and English is that in English intonation functions at the sentence level instead of the word level, with the rises and falls of the sentence conveying the emotional impact of the message. The problem for Westerners learning Chinese is not hearing intonation per se, but hearing intonation as part of the pronunciation of a word.

The tones of Putonghua

In Putonghua, most words are pronounced with one of four tones. (Some unaccented syllables are also pronounced with a "light" tone — more about this later.) Tones 1, 2, and 4 are relatively straightforward, so not too much need be said about them. Tone 3 changes according to what follows it, so will require greater elaboration. Let's look at them one by one:

Tone 1

Tone #1 is a high level pitch, like singing a long high note.

Tone 1

Tone 2

Tone #2 is a rising tone, like the word "yes" used as a question in answering the door: "Yes?"

Tone 2

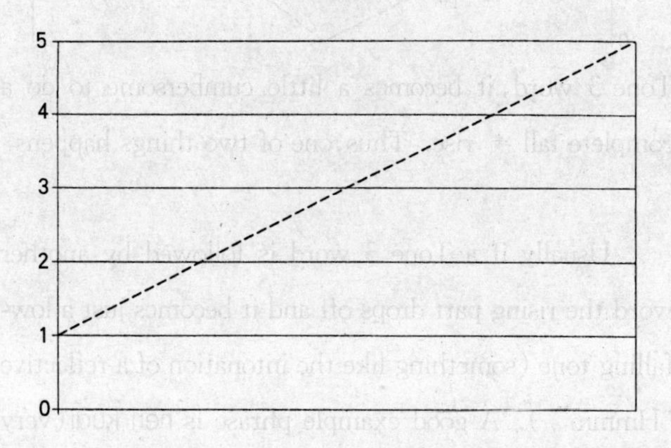

Tone 3

Tone #3 is usually described as a "falling-rising" tone, and this is what it sounds like when a word is pronounced in isolation or at the end of a sentence. However, you will find that if another word follows a

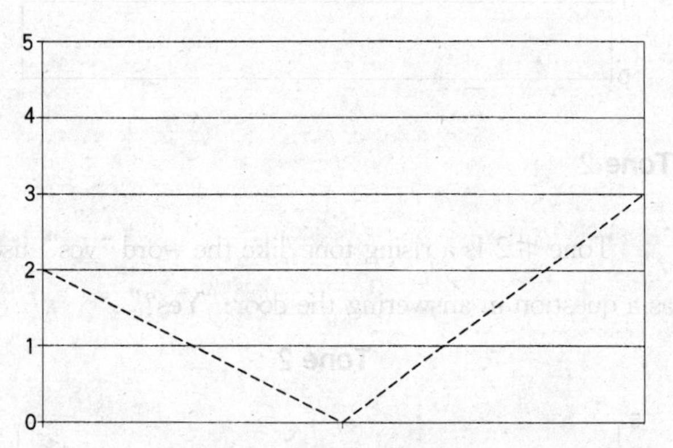

Tone 3 word, it becomes a little cumbersome to do a complete fall + rise. Thus, one of two things happens.

Usually if a Tone 3 word is followed by another word the rising part drops off and it becomes just a low-falling tone (something like the intonation of a reflective "Hmmm"). A good example phrase is hěn kuài (very fast).

Tone 3 (followed by most words)

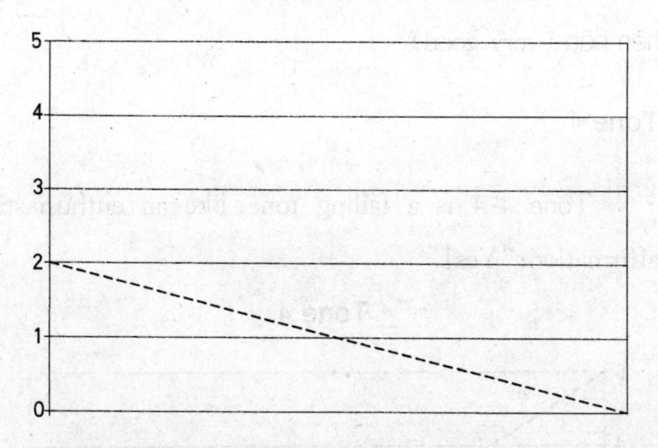

But (and here is the tricky part), when one Tone 3 word is followed by another Tone 3 word, the tone of the first word changes to a rising tone (just like Tone 2). Essentially, it is the initial falling part of the tone

Tone 3 (followed by another Tone 3)

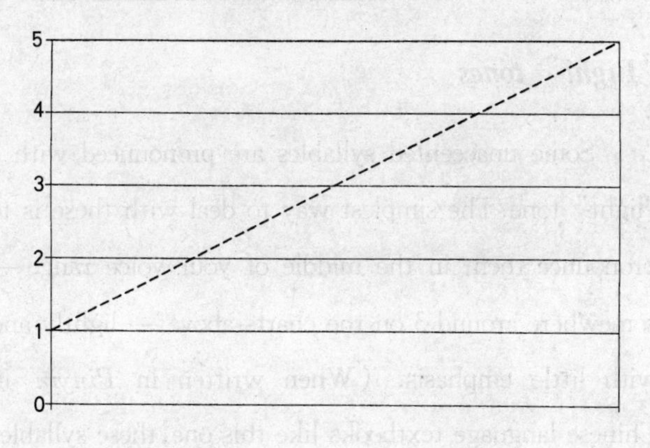

which is now omitted. A good example phrase for this is hěn hǎo (very good).

Tone 4

Tone #4 is a falling tone, like an enthusiastic affirmation: "Yes!"

Tone 4

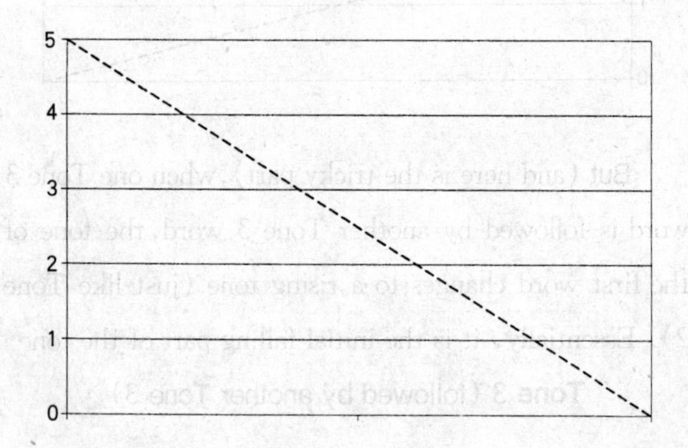

"*Light*" *tones*

Some unaccented syllables are pronounced with a "light" tone. The simplest way to deal with these is to pronounce them in the middle of your voice range — somewhere around 3 on the charts above — lightly and with little emphasis. (When written in *Pinyin* in Chinese language textbooks like this one, these syllables have no tone mark over them.)

Learning tones

The natural assumption when first confronted with all these tones is that you need to memorize which tone category each new Chinese word belongs to, i.e. which word is a Tone 1, which is a Tone 2 and so forth. However, as you will quickly discover, trying to recall information in this format when you are trying to say a sentence isn't very efficient; when talking you don't have time to be constantly asking yourself "Is this word pronounced with the first or fourth tone?" It needs to come out naturally and quickly. So, what should you do?

One bit of advice is to start with your ears. When Chinese children learn to speak, nobody teaches them which words are Tone 3 and so forth. Rather they listen and learn to say what sounds right. Likewise, to get your tones right without stopping to think before every word, you need to go with what sounds right. However, before you can do this you need to train yourself to listen carefully to the pronunciation of new words, including their tone. As your tutor pronounces new Chinese words, try to fix the intonation in your mind along with the pronunciation. Perhaps even ask your tutor to exaggerate the tone a little when pronouncing new words for you — making it funny may help you remember it better.

A second suggestion is practice, lots of it. The first few times you say anything new, it requires conscious thought, and you may well need to pause to remember which words are pronounced with which tones. However, after you have said a certain word, word combination or phrase a few times, it starts to become automatic and you don't need to think about it so much (thus freeing your attention for other problems). Don't practice things just to the point where you can scrape your way through them once; practice until you can do them without thinking.

Finally, don't become overly concerned about tones. Yes, you should try to get them right, but you shouldn't become so worried that you are reluctant to speak. Remember, Chinese people will often understand you quite well even if your tones are wrong, especially if you speak in phrases rather than single words (If you speak in single word utterances and get the tone wrong, it may be more difficult for Chinese to understand, especially if the situation or context doesn't make it easy for the listener to guess what you might be trying to say). It is much better to get a sentence out with the tones wrong than not to open you mouth at all. As long as you keep speaking — and keep paying attention to how things sound when Chinese people say them — the accuracy of your tones and naturalness of your pronunciation will continue to improve.

Lesson 1: Buying (I)

In this lesson: *Asking prices. Numbers. Greetings, courtesy phrases. Yes/no question pattern. Signs: bathrooms, exits.*

Core Lesson

Dialogue

The first task most foreigners need to accomplish in Chinese is making a purchase. Below, A is a hesitant foreigner pointing to something in a store. B is a Chinese store clerk.

(The English translation in parentheses after each Pinyin line is a literal word-by-word translation of the Chinese. For a more natural English translation, see

the end of the lesson.)

A：Duōshao qián? (How much money?)
多少钱?

B：Sān kuài. (Three *yuan*.)
三块。

B：Nǐ yào bú yào? (You want not want?)
你要不要?

A：Bú yào. (Not want.)
不要。

Dialogue Vocabulary

duōshao(how much)多少
qián(money)钱
sān(three)三
kuài(Chinese dollar, *yuan*)块
nǐ(you)你
yào (to want)要
bù(not, no)不

Additional Vocabulary

qǐng(please)请
wèn(to ask)问
zhè(this)这
zàijiàn(goodbye)再见
xièxie(thank you)谢谢
duì(right, correct)对

gè(*measure word*)个

hǎo(good)好

zǎo(early; good morning)早

hěn(very)很

guì(expensive)贵

piányi(inexpensive)便宜

***Numbers*:**

yī(one)一

èr (two, *ordinal — used in counting*)二

sān(three)三

sì(four)四

wǔ(five)五

liù(six)六

qī(seven)七

bā(eight)八

jiǔ(nine)九

shí(ten)十

bǎi(hundred)百

qiān(thousand)千

liǎng(two, *cardinal*, *see "Notes"*)两

Useful Phrases

- Nǐ hǎo.

  (You good?)

  = How are you?

This is the most common Chinese greeting. To respond, simply say "Nǐ hǎo" *back*. Hǎo *used by itself often also means "Okay."*

- Zǎo.

  (Early)

  = Good morning.

- Zàijiàn.

  (Again see.)

  = Good-bye.

- Xièxie.

  (Thanks.)

Sentence Patterns

How do I state a price?

Pattern: (amount) + (measure word) + qián (money).

Examples :

— liǎng kuài qián(two pieces of money) = 2 yuan

— bā kuài qián(eight pieces of money) = 8 yuan

In daily speech, the word qián *(money) is often omitted, but the measure word will not normally be omitted. Thus, for "eight dollars" you will often hear* bā kuài, *but never* * bā qián. Kuài *is the colloquial* *measure word for "dollar" (yuan). (See "Notes" for more on measure words.)*

How do I ask a yes/no question?

One common pattern for yes/no questions is:

Pattern: (verb/adjective) + bù (not) + (verb/adjective).

Examples:

— Nǐ yào bú yào (You want not want) = Do you want this or not?

— Nǐ hǎo bù hǎo (You good not good) = Are you okay or not?

— Hǎo bù hǎo? (Okay not okay?) = Is this okay?

How do I make a question more polite?

Pattern: Qǐng wèn + (question).

Examples :

— Qǐng wèn, zhè ge duōshao qián? (Please let me ask, this how much?)

A question prefaced with Qǐng wèn is much more polite than one that is not.

Notes

Duōshao:

Duō means "many" and shǎo means "few." (When these are combined, shǎo loses its tone and become a "light tone" syllable.)

Numbers:

Larger numbers in Chinese are delightfully logical.

— Numbers from 11 – 19: shí(10) + number. Ex: 15 = shí wǔ.

— Multiples of 10: (number) + shí. Ex: 30 = sān shí.

— From 21 – 29: èr shí(20) + number. Ex: 21 = èr shí yī, and so forth. The same for larger numbers. For example, 86 = bā shí liù.

— Hundreds: 100 is yī bǎi, 200 is liǎng bǎi, and so forth.

— Thousands: 1,000 is yī qiān, 2,000 is liǎng qiān and so forth.

Èr *and* liǎng:

Chinese has two words for "two."

— Èr is used in counting and in names of larger numbers. Ex: èr shí èr = 22.

— Liǎng is used when you are talking about two of something. Ex: Liǎng gè rén = two people.

— 20 is always èr shí.

— 200 is normally èr bǎi, but you will also hear people use liǎng bǎi.

— 2,000 is normally liǎng qiān, but you will also hear èr qiān.

Bù:

The word bù is normally pronounced with a falling (4th) tone, but you may notice that when your tutor says yào bú yào, the bù in the middle doesn't fall; rather it is pronounced with a rising tone or only a light tone. The rule is that if bù is followed by another 4th tone word, it becomes a rising tone. (This tends to happen naturally.) Do not fear — most Tone 4 words do not do this.

Measure words:

In Chinese, between a number and a noun you always need to add a measure word. A measure word is like the word "cups" in the English phrase "three cups of water," a word that indicates the general kind or quantity of whatever object is being discussed. The difference between English and Chinese is that whereas English only requires measure words for mass nouns (Ex: two bags of rice, three pounds of pork, etc.), Chinese always requires a measure word between numbers and nouns. In this lesson we have the measure word kuài (literally "piece" but also means *yuan*); above we also see the measure word gè in the phrase liǎng gè rén (two people). We will encounter more measure words in the lessons to come.

Tip: Listening to Chinese on the street.

Listening comprehension in a foreign language involves a lot of guessing, as you will no doubt discover when you try the material in today's lesson in a real Chinese store. People don't talk like scripts in a Chinese textbook. Instead, they speak in incomplete sentences, don't always enunciate slowly and clearly, and frequently use words you haven't learned yet. Also, not everyone in China speaks standard Putonghua of the kind taught in classrooms and spoken on TV; in fact, many Chinese learn Putonghua as a second language, and their first language is some Chinese dialect which is only more or less distantly related to Putonghua.

("Putonghua" literally means "common language" and is the name of the Chinese dialect used as the official national language in China. It is also known as "Mandarin Chinese" because for centuries it was the language used by China's officials. Most Chinese speak some variant of Putonghua as their first language, and all over China it is the language generally used in schools, the media, and most interaction between people of different regions.)

The first step toward success in Chinese listening comprehension is accepting this situation as normal rather than wasting emotional energy agonizing over it. The second is developing the habit of just wading in and guessing, using any clues you have. Start by trying to hear the numbers as you ask prices in local stores.

Practice Ideas

Practice with a tutor

***Listening practice*:**

Have your tutor randomly say numbers between 1 and 10 while you respond by raising the appropriate number of fingers. The tutor says "Correct"(duì) if you are right, "Wrong"(bú duì) if you are wrong. Over time, work for greater speed; speed of recognition of numbers is vital when you get out into real stores.

***Saying numbers*:**

To practice saying numbers, do the drill above with roles reversed, with you saying the numbers and trying to make the tutor understand.

***Saying numbers*:**

To practice generating larger numbers and saying them correctly, have your tutor write down numbers in Arabic script; you then say the number in Chinese. Do this drill repeatedly over a number of days to build speed and accuracy.

***Tone / Pinyin practice*:**

Have your tutor say Chinese numbers at random while you listen and then write down the *Pinyin* (Romanization) and/or the tones. This is good practice for both your listening skills and *Pinyin*. You can do the same exercise pointing to objects in the room as a way to build vocabulary while practicing your listening and *Pinyin*.

***Role-play*:**

Practice buying and selling with you as the buyer and your tutor as the seller. Pointing to objects in the room, ask your tutor how much it costs. The tutor names a price and you pay (using real Chinese money would be very useful practice). For fun you could also comment "Too expensive!" (Tài guì) or "Very cheap!" (Hěn piányi) as appropriate.

***Reading*:**

Have your tutor write out numbers in random order in Chinese characters; you then read them.

Alternatively, use flash cards.

***Writing*:**

Ask your tutor to show you the proper stroke order for writing the Chinese characters for the Vocabulary, starting with the numbers.

***Taping*:**

Have your tutor tape the Dialogue and other parts of the lesson for you.

Practice on the street

***Real life practice* (*RLP*):**

Use your newly-acquired Chinese skills to buy something in a local store. Before buying, ask the price. (If you have a tutor with you, insist that he/she let you talk for yourself, intervening only when you get beyond your depth and request assistance.)

***Field trip*:**

Ask a friend or tutor to show you where to buy things you need nearby.

***Sign reading*:**

As you walk around your area, try to locate Chinese numbers on signs. See if you can find all of the numbers from 1 to 10. Also look for bathrooms (see Survival Characters below).

Extra Credit

Survival Characters

Chinese "sign literacy" should probably begin with the characters that help you find the appropriate bathroom, with the character for "exit" thrown in for good measure:

女 nǚ (woman; women's) 男 nán (man; men's)

厕所 cèsuǒ (toilet, bathroom) 出口 chūkǒu (exit)

Colloquial translation of Dialogue

A: How much (does this) cost?

B: Three dollars.

B: Do you want it?

A: No, I don't.

Lesson 2: In The Cafeteria

In this lesson: "*What is this?*" *Flavors. Yes/no questions. Compliments and polite responses. Signs: cafeteria menus.*

Core Lesson

Dialogue

A is a curious and hungry foreigner looking at food in a Chinese cafeteria. B, the Chinese server, patiently answers questions.

A: Zhè shì shénme? (This is what?)

这是什么?

B: Zhè shì jī. (This is chicken.)

这是鸡。

A：Zhè gè ne?（This?）

这个呢?

B：Yú. Nǐ chī ma?（Fish. You eat?）

鱼。你吃吗?

A：Chī.（Eat.）

吃。

B：Nǐ de Hànyǔ hěn hǎo.（Your Chinese very good.）

你的汉语很好。

A：Nǎli, nǎli.（Where, where.）= Oh no, not really.

哪里，哪里。

Dialogue Vocabulary

zhè(this)这

shì(is)是

shénme(what)什么

jī(chicken)鸡

gè(*measure word*)个

ne(*question marker*)呢

yú(fish)鱼

chī(to eat)吃

ma(*question marker*)吗

de(*possessive marker*)的

Hànyǔ(Chinese language)汉语

hěn(very)很

hǎo(good)好

nǎli(where)哪里

Additional Vocabulary

xián(salty)咸　　tián(sweet)甜

là(spicy hot)辣　　wǒ(I, me)我

tīng(to listen)听　　dǒng(to understand)懂

duì(right, correct)对

Useful Phrases

- Xián bù xián?

  (Salty or not?)

Also:

— Tián bù tián? (Sweet or not?)

— Là bú là? (Spicy hot or not?)

- Wǒ tīng bù dǒng.

  (I hear not understand.)

  = I don't understand.

- Hǎo chī.

  (Good to eat.)

  = Tastes good!

Bù hǎo chī is the opposite.

Sentence Patterns

What is the word order for asking — and answering — "What is this?"

Pattern: Zhè(this) + shì(is) + shénme(what).

Examples:

— Zhè shì shénme? (This is what?) = What is this?

— Zhè shì jī. (This is chicken.)

— Zhè shì qián. (This is money.)

Notice that the word order for this question is the opposite of the order in English, and that the same word order is used for both question and answer.

How do I ask a yes/no question (II)?

A second common way to ask yes/no questions is by adding ma to the end of a statement.

Pattern: Zhè(this) + shì(is) + (noun) + ma(question marker).

Examples:

— Zhè shì yú ma? (This is fish?) = Is this fish?

— Zhè shì qián ma? (This is money?) = Is this

money?

— Zhè shì nǐ de ma? (This is yours?) = Is this yours?

How do I answer a yes/no question?

To answer affirmatively to a yes/no question, repeat the verb. To answer negatively, repeat the verb with a bù in front of it.

Examples:

A: Nǐ chī bù chī? (You eat not eat?) = Are you going to eat it?

B: Chī. (Eat.) = Yes.

A: Nǐ ne? (You?) = And you?

C: Bù chī. (Not eat.) = No.

Notes

Shénme:

The "n" in this word is silent. This is one of the very few Chinese words not pronounced exactly as the *Pinyin* spelling would indicate.

Measure words:

In Lesson 1 we saw that between numbers and

nouns a measure word is required. In the Dialogue above we see that a measure word is also usually required after zhè (this).

Gè:

This is the most common measure word in Chinese, and when you are in doubt as to what measure word to use, gè will get you by.

Ne:

Ne is a question marker, but it is only used for brief follow-up questions in situations where context already makes the question clear. So, for example, instead of asking the whole question Zhè shì shénme? several times in a row as you point to different items in a store, for the follow-up questions you could ask Zhè gè ne? (Ne sentences would often be translated in English as "How about ____?")

De:

De marks possession. Thus:

— Wǒ de = My/mine.

— Nǐ de = Your/yours.

— Tā de= His/hers.

Nǎli *and compliments*:

The normal polite Chinese response to a compliment is to deny it, and this is often done with the phrase Nǎli, nǎli, which literally means "Where? Where?" but would better be translated something like "Oh no, not really!" (As in the Dialogue above, Chinese people will often compliment even the most feeble attempts foreigners make to speak Chinese.)

Strategy*: *Controlling conversations with questions.

In early stages of Chinese practice on the streets, a good way to give yourself a fighting chance to understand what Chinese people say to you is by controlling the conversation with questions that help you predict what you might hear in response. Zhè shì shénme? (What is this?) is one very useful question because it both generates predictable responses and new vocabulary. Yes/no questions are also good because they limit the possible responses.

Tip: ***Grammar.***

Learning Chinese grammar is largely a question of remembering word order. (This is the main reason why Chinese word order is preserved as much as possible in the English translations of the Dialogue sentences, even when the result is pidgin English.) For example, note that the word order in Zhè shì shénme? (This is what?) is the opposite of English "What is this?"

Practice Ideas

Practice with a tutor

Review:

Use activities from Lesson 1 to review numbers and buying. Try to build your speed and accuracy. You should review numbers until you can say and recognize them quickly and confidently; continue to review them for several days or longer.

***Tone/Pinyin practice*:**

To generate new vocabulary while practicing your *Pinyin*, point at objects around the room (or objects you have brought with you) and ask your tutor Zhè shì shénme? As the tutor answers, write down the new words in *Pinyin*. Check by pointing to the object and identifying it saying: Zhè shì ____; your tutor responds with Duì/Bú duì or Hǎo/bù hǎo. Make it a game and try to build for speed. Keep notes of useful new words you learn in a little notebook you can easily carry around with you. (You might also ask the tutor to check your *Pinyin*, but keep in mind that most Chinese rarely use *Pinyin*.)

***Tone/Pinyin practice*:**

Ask your tutor to dictate words for things you like to eat.

***Role play*:**

Following the model of the Dialogue, you play the role of customer in a cafeteria and your tutor plays the server. Point to dishes, ask what they are, ask how much they cost, and decide whether or not to take them. Use real Chinese money so that you get used to handling it quickly — the more familiar you are with Chinese money, the less traumatic buying things will be.

***Reading*:**

Have your tutor write characters from the lesson on cards, either all of them or just the "Survival Characters" (below), and then do a flash card drill with you.

Practice on the street

***Real life practice* (*RLP*):**

Try ordering a meal in a cafeteria. Ask what kinds of dishes are offered, whether they are sweet/salty/hot, and whether they are good to eat. Score brownie points with the staff by later complimenting the food (Hǎo chī!).

***RLP*:**

Try buying a snack food in a local store. Before buying, ask whether it is sweet/salty/hot, and ask the price. If anyone compliments your Chinese, remember to respond with Nǎli, nǎli. If you start getting overwhelmed with Chinese you can't understand, escape with Wǒ tīng bù dǒng (I don't understand).

***Field trip*:**

Ask your tutor to show you a few good local eateries. While there, look at a menu (which may be written on the wall or on a blackboard) and try to locate your new survival characters.

Extra Credit

Survival Characters

It will no doubt be some time before you can read a Chinese menu, but even knowing a few characters can get you started guessing what might be in a dish in a Chinese restaurant or cafeteria. Chinese dishes are often distinguished by what meat they contain, so the characters below are a good place to start.

鸡 jī(chicken) 猪 zhū(pig, pork)

鱼 yú(fish)　　肉 ròu(meat, usually pork unless other-
牛 niú(cow, beef)　wise specified)

Extra Credit Vocabulary

A few more basic food items:

jī dàn(chicken eggs)鸡蛋　miàn(noodles)面
shūcài(vegetables)蔬菜　fàn(rice)饭

Colloquial translation of Dialogue

A: What is this?
B: This is chicken.
A: What about this?
B: Fish. Want to eat some?
A: Yes.

Lesson 3: Buying (II)

In this lesson: "*Do you have any ____?*" *Daily necessity items.* "*What does ____ mean?*" *Chinese character radicals.*

Core Lesson

Dialogue

Emboldened by the success of her/his visit in Lesson 1, A has returned to the Chinese store for another purchase. B is still the clerk.

A: Yǒu méiyǒu xìnfēng? (Have not have envelopes?)
有没有信封?

B: Yǒu. Yào jǐ gè? (Have. Want how many?)

有。要几个？

A：Bā gè. Yǒu méiyǒu yóupiào?（Eight. Have not have stamps?）

八个。有没有邮票？

B：Duìbuqǐ，méiyǒu.（Sorry，don't have.）

对不起，没有。

A：Bā gè xìnfēng duōshao qián?（Eight envelopes how much?）

八个信封多少钱？

B：Liù máo yí gè. Sì kuài bā.（*60* cents for one. $ *4.80*.）

六毛一个。四块八。

Dialogue Vocabulary

yǒu（have）有

méiyǒu（not have）没有

xìn（letter）信

xìnfēng（envelope）信封

jǐ（how many；several）几

gè（*measure word*）个

yóupiào（stamp）邮票

duìbuqǐ（sorry；excuse me）对不起

Additional Vocabulary

yìsi(meaning)意思

Other items you may need to buy:

féizào(soap)肥皂 yágāo(toothpaste)牙膏

zhǐ(paper)纸 bǐ(pen)笔

xìnzhǐ(letter paper)信纸 qiānbǐ(pencil)铅笔

wèishēngzhǐ(toilet paper)卫生纸

xǐfàshuǐ(shampoo; *lit.* wash hair water)洗发水

Useful Phrases

- Shénme yìsi?

  (What meaning?)

  = What does it mean?

Sentence Patterns

How do I ask "Do you have any ____?"

Pattern: Yǒu méiyǒu + (item)?

Examples:

— Yǒu méiyǒu xìnfēng? (Have not have envelopes?) = Do you have any envelopes?

— Yǒu méiyǒu yóupiào? (Have not have stamps?) = Do you have any stamps?

— Yǒu méiyǒu yú? (Have not have fish?) = Do you have any fish?

This pattern is used for asking if someone has something, whether or not something is available, or even whether or not something exists.

How do I ask "How much do/does ____ cost?"

Pattern: (item) + duōshao qián?

Examples:

— Xìnfēng duōshao qián? (Envelopes how much money?) = How much do envelopes cost?

— Yóupiào duōshao qián? (Stamps how much money?) = How much do stamps cost?

How do I ask "What does ____ mean?"

Pattern: (unfamiliar word) + shì + shénme yìsi?

Examples:

— "Xìnfēng" shì shénme yìsi? (Xìnfēng is what meaning?) = What does xìnfēng mean?

Notes

Yǒu méiyǒu:

This "have/not have" construction is used where in English you would say "Do you have any ____?" or "Are there any ____?" (It also has other uses: Nǐ yǒu méiyǒu chī fàn? is one way to say "Have you eaten yet?")

***Plurals*:**

In the Dialogue above you will notice that Chinese makes no distinction between the singular and plural forms of most nouns. For example, xìnfēng means both "envelope" and "envelopes." Whether or not something is singular or plural is determined from context.

Jǐ ***and*** zhǐ:

Notice that the pronunciation of "-i" in these two words is different. See "Guide to *Pinyin* and Pronunciation" for explanation.

Duōshao ***and*** jǐ:

— Duōshao is used for asking about bulk amounts and large quantities of things (Rule of thumb:

more than ten); it does not take a measure word. Ex: Duōshao qián? = How much money?

— Jǐ is used for smaller numbers of things and is almost always used with a measure word. Ex: Jǐ kuài qián? = How many dollars?

— Jǐ can also mean "several." Ex: Wǒ yào jǐ gè xìnfēng = I would like several envelopes.

Strategy: Reading Chinese on the street.

Reading, like listening, is a guessing game in which you use whatever clues you have to get the information you need. You will not be reading Chinese novels soon, but you can already start using the characters you know to unlock the secrets of Chinese maps, signs, menus, and so forth. If you get into the habit of looking at the written Chinese around you in daily life, you will not only review the characters you already know, but also notice new ones that appear frequently and beg you to learn them. Carry a little notebook so you can copy down characters you want to learn.

Practice Ideas

Practice with a tutor

Review:

Practice buying and selecting food at a cafeteria.

Listening practice:

Have your tutor say prices while you either write them down or produce the appropriate sum of money. Practice until you can respond quickly.

Tone/Pinyin listening practice:

Ask your tutor to make a list of words unfamiliar to you. Then the tutor says the words aloud and you try to write down what you hear (both pronunciation and tone) in *Pinyin*. If you want to know the meaning of a new word, ask by saying ____ shì shénme yìsi? (What does ____ mean?)

Role play:

Make a shopping list. Then ask the storekeeper

(your tutor) whether or not he/she has the items and what they cost.

Practice on the street

***RLP*:**

Go to a store to buy toothpaste, toilet paper, etc. Begin by asking if they have the item, and then ask the price. If things go well, point out a few other items and ask what they are.

***Field trip*:**

Ask a Chinese friend to show you where to buy stationery, stamps, or other daily necessities.

***Sign reading*:**

Look on signs for characters containing the radicals introduced below.

Extra Credit

Survival Characters

Most Chinese characters are made up of basic building blocks called radicals. These radicals often give clues to either the pronunciation or meaning of a character, especially as you reach advanced stages of Chinese study. (They can also be confusing, as in the case of the water radical in the character 没.) However, even at the beginning stages, learning to see and pay attention to radicals will help you remember Chinese characters more efficiently.

Several of the most common radicals appear at the left hand side or top of characters in this lesson. In each case, see if you can guess why the radical is part of this particular character. (Note: the first three are relatively easy to figure out, the fourth is considerably more obscure, and the last may even confuse your tutor.)

— The gold/metal radical is the left side of 钱

— The silk radical is the left side of 纸

— The bamboo radical is at the top of 笔

— The single person radical is the left side of 信

— The water radical is the left hand side of 没

Colloquial translation of Dialogue

A: Do you have any envelopes?

B: Yes. How many do you want?

A: Eight. Do you have any stamps?

B: Sorry, we don't.

A: How much for eight envelopes?

B: Sixty cents apiece. $4.80 (total).

Lesson 4: Post Office (I)

In this lesson: *Mailing letters, buying stamps. Countries. Signs: post office services.*

Core Lesson

Dialogue

A is handing two unstamped letters to a B, a clerk in a post office.

B: Jì dào nǎli? (Send to where?)
寄到哪里?

A: Jiānádà. (To Canada.)
加拿大。

A: Jì dào Jiānádà duōshao qián? (Send to Canada

how much?)

寄到加拿大多少钱?

B: Dào Jiānádà sì kuài èr. (To Canada $4.20.)

到加拿大四块二。

B: Jǐ fēng xìn? (How many letters?)

几封信?

A: Liǎng fēng. (Two letters.)

两封。

A: Wǒ zài mǎi wǔ gè sì kuài èr de yóupiào. (I also buy five $4.20 stamps.)

我再买五个四块二的邮票。

Dialogue Vocabulary

jì(to mail)寄

nǎli(where)哪里

fēng(*measure word for letters*)封

zài(again, also)再

dào(to)到

Jiānádà(Canada) 加拿大

wǒ(I, me)我

mǎi(to buy)买

Additional Vocabulary

ná(to get, to take, to carry) 拿

fā chuánzhēn(to send a fax)
发传真

bāoguǒ(package)
包裹

gěi(to give)给

tài(too)太

Useful Phrases

- Wǒ yào ná bāoguǒ.
  (I want get package.)
  = I want to get a package.

- Wǒ yào fā chuánzhēn.
  (I want send fax.)
  = I want to send a fax.

Sentence Patterns

How do I ask to buy stamps of a certain cost (Like "$ 4.20 stamps")?

This pattern is complicated but it is worth learning if you need to buy stamps and other items denominated by price.

Pattern: Wǒ yào + (number of items) + (measure word) + (cost) + de + (item).

Examples:

— Wǒ yào liǎng gè sān kuài qián de yóupiào. (I want two 3.00 dollars' stamps.) = I want two 3 *yuan* stamps.

— Wǒ yào mǎi shí gè sān kuài liù de yóupiào. (I want buy ten 3 dollar 60's stamps.) = I want to buy ten 3.60 *yuan* stamps.

Notes

***Measure words*:**

Notice in the Dialogue that when giving a short answer like "two letters" you say liǎng fēng, not * liǎng xìn. The pattern is (number) + (measure word), not (number) + (object).

Nǎli:

In northern China you will hear nǎr instead of nǎli. Northern Chinese add "r" ending to many words.

***Tip*: *Practice makes perfect*.**

By now you may be getting tired of practicing numbers and buying. However, in language study there is much to be said for practicing something until you can do it rapidly and almost automatically. One of the arts of language learning is finding variations on basic forms of practice so that you can get the repetition you need without becoming so bored that your mind switches off.

Practice Ideas

Practice with a tutor

***Review*:**

Review purchasing things at a store.

***Listening practice*:**

Ask your tutor to say large numbers as you try to write them down.

***Word usage practice*:**

Make up a few sentences for your tutor using liǎng and èr to see if you understand which to use where.

***Role play*:**

With your tutor, role play mailing a letter and buying stamps at the post office.

***Reading*:**

Ask your tutor to write out a dialogue similar to but not exactly the same as the one above, then you practice reading. This provides valuable practice in reading handwritten Chinese characters. Use the question "Zhè shì shénme yìsi?" to ask about unfamiliar words.

Practice on the street

***RLP*:**

Go to the post office and ask how much it costs to send a letter to your home country. Better yet, take an unstamped letter, find out how much it costs, and mail it.

***RLP*:**

Buy stamps at the post office. Some stores also sell stamps, especially the denominations most often used locally, and you may find that buying at a small store is less stressful.

***Field trip*:**

Ask a Chinese friend to take you to a nearby post office and show you where to buy stamps, pick up packages, etc.

Extra Credit

Survival Characters

These are useful characters to know for signs in the post office.

邮局 yóujú(post office)　　邮票 yóupiào(stamps)
包裹 bāoguǒ(package)　　信件 xìnjiàn(letters)

Extra Credit Vocabulary

Countries: These are some country names you might find useful.

Ài'ěrlán(Ireland)爱尔兰　　Àodàlìyà(Australia)澳大利亚
Dānmài(Denmark)丹麦
Éguó(Russia)俄国　　Déguó(Germany)德国

Fēilǜbīn(Phillippines)菲律宾
Hánguó(Korea)韩国
Jiānádà(Canada)加拿大
Nuówēi(Norway)挪威
Ruìdiǎn(Sweden)瑞典
Xīnxīlán(New Zealand)新西兰
Yīngguó(England)英国
Yìdàlì(Italy)意大利
Fǎguó(France)法国
Fēnlán(Finland)芬兰
Hélán(Holland)荷兰
Měiguó(America)美国
Rìběn(Japan)日本
Sūgélán(Scotland)苏格兰

Colloquial translation of Dialogue

B: Where do you want to send this?

A: Canada. How much does it cost to Canada?

B: It costs $4.20 to Canada. How many letters?

A: Two. I'll also buy five $4.20 stamps.

Lesson 5: Asking Directions

In this lesson: "*Where is ____?*" *Location, direction, distance. Signs: basic place and street name characters.*

Core Lesson

Dialogue

A needs directions to the post office.

A: Qǐng wèn, yóujú zài nǎli? (May I ask, the post office is where?)
请问,邮局在哪里?

B: Zài qiánmian. (Up ahead.)
在前面。

A：Yuǎn bù yuǎn?（Far or not?）

远不远?

B：Bù yuǎn, hěn jìn.（Not far, very near.）

不远，很近。

A：Zài zuǒbian ma?（On left side?）

在左边吗?

B：Bú shì. Zài yòubian.（Not is. On right side.）

不是。在右边。

Dialogue Vocabulary

qǐng(please)请

wèn(to ask)问

yóujú(post office)邮局

zài(at, on, in, etc.)在

qiánmian(ahead)前面

yuǎn(far)远

jìn(near)近

zuǒbian(left side)左边

yòubian(right side)右边

Additional Vocabulary

cèsuǒ(toilet, bathroom) 厕所

xǐshǒujiān(washroom) 洗手间

hòumian(behind)后面

duìmiàn(opposite side)对面

lǐmiàn(inside)里面

wàimian(outside)外面

shūdiàn(bookstore)书店

chāojí shìchǎng(supermarket)超级市场

bǎihuò shāngdiàn(department store)百货商店

Useful Phrases

- Hànyǔ zénme shuō?

  (Chinese how say?)

  = How do you say this in Chinese?

Best used while pointing at something.

Sentence Patterns

How do I ask "Where is ____?"

Pattern: (place) + zài nǎli.

Examples:

— Shūdiàn zài nǎli? (Bookstore is where?) = Where is the bookstore?

— Cèsuǒ zài nǎli? (Bathroom is where?) = Where is the bathroom?

— Xǐshǒujiān zài nǎli? (Wash-hand-room is where?) = Where is the bathroom?

— Xǐshǒujiān *is a more delicate term than the*

workaday cèsuǒ.

How do I say "*the bookstore is ahead*"?

Pattern: (destination) + zài + (direction).

Example:

— Shūdiàn zài qiánmian. (Bookstore is ahead.) = The bookstore is ahead.

Note that qiánmian *must come at the end in this pattern, unlike English word order in which "Ahead is the bookstore" is also possible.*

How do I say "*there is a bookstore ahead*"?

Pattern: (direction) + yǒu + (place).

Example:

— Qiánmian yǒu shūdiàn. (Ahead there is bookstore.)

The yǒu *here is the same* yǒu (*to have, to exist*) *that we met in Lesson* 3.

Notes

Zài:

In Chinese one preposition of place, zài, covers everything — in, on, at, etc.

***Strategies*: *Asking directions*.**

You won't be able to understand a complicated set of directions in Chinese any time in the near future, but if you can ask where something is, people can always point you in the right direction. A yes/no question like yuǎn bù yuǎn? also has a good chance of prompting a response that you can understand.

Practice Ideas

Practice with a tutor

***Review*:**

Role play mailing a letter.

***Tone / Pinyin practice*:**

(If your tutor knows English) Using the ____ Hànyǔ zénme shuō? question, ask your tutor how to say the following items in Chinese: chocolate, coke, cookies, tea, ice cream, shoes, towels, shampoo, cup or whatever else you might want or need. Listen carefully and try to write down the words in *Pinyin*. (Add useful ones to your vocabulary notebook.)

***Tone/Pinyin practice*:**

In Chinese, ask your tutor how to say the names of a few places you might want to go to: park, front gate, whatever.

***Role play*:**

Using the Qǐng wèn, ____ zài nǎli? question, practice asking where places are.

***Game*: "*Hot and cold*."**

Have your tutor hide something while you are out of the room. When you return, have him/her guide you to the object saying yuǎn and jìn instead of "hot" and "cold." Then add qiánmian, hòumian, yòubian, and zuǒbian. This will help you memorize vocabulary (and also entertain your tutor).

***Map reading*:**

Get a Chinese map of the city, and using the ____ zài nǎli? question, find out where a few important places are. Also look for the Survival Characters listed below.

***Reading*:**

Have your tutor write out a few sentences or a dialogue using the words you know, then practice reading it.

Practice on the street

***RLP*:**

Look for things in your city (department store, bookstore, etc.), using the Qǐng wèn, ____ zài nǎli? question to ask people as you go. Better yet, turn your outing into a treasure hunt by having your tutor give you a list of things to find and the necessary vocabulary.

***RLP*:**

List the Chinese names of items you wish to buy, and then go to a department store. Locate the items by asking clerks where they are.

***Field trip*:**

Ask a Chinese friend to help you find a Chinese map of the city.

***Sign reading*:**

On street signs, look for the Survival Characters (below).

Extra Credit

Survival Characters

Chinese maps may seem intimidating, but you can learn a surprising amount from them even only knowing a few Chinese characters. On city maps, the following characters are among those that appear most frequently, often in street names. You will also see these characters on maps of China because they appear in many province and place names.

东 dōng(east)	南 nán(south)
西 xī(west)	北 běi(north)
山 shān(mountain)	江 jiāng(river)
湖 hú(lake)	河 hé(river)

Colloquial translation of Dialogue

A: Excuse me, where's the post office?

B: Up ahead.

A: Is it far?

B: No, it's very close.

A: Is it on the left?

B: No, it's on the right.

Lesson 6: Introducing Yourself

In this lesson: "*Which country are you from?*" "*What do you do?*" *Names.* "*Where do you ____?*" *City maps: common locations.*

Core Lesson

Dialogue

A is a curious Chinese student who has encountered foreigner B and B's two companions at a store. A strikes up a conversation.

A: Qǐng wèn, nǐ shì cóng nǎ gè guójiā lái de? (Please ask, you are from which country come?)

请问，你是从哪个国家来的？

B：Wǒ shì cóng Yīngguó lái de.（I am from England come.）

我是从英国来的。

A：Nǐ zài Zhōngguó zuò shénme?（You in China do what?）

你在中国做什么？

B：Wǒ zài Nánjīng Dàxué jiāo Yīngyǔ.（I at Nanjing University teach English.）

我在南京大学教英语。

A：Tāmen ne?（Them?）

他们呢？

B：Tāmen shì Měiguó rén.（They are Americans.）

他们是美国人。

B：Tāmen zài Nán Dà xué Hànyǔ.（They at Nanjing University study Chinese.）

他们在南大学汉语。

Dialogue Vocabulary

cóng(from)从　　nǎ(which)哪

guójiā(country)国家　　lái(to come)来

Yīngguó(England)英国　　Zhōngguó(China)中国

zuò(to do)做

Nánjīng(Nanjing)南京

dàxué(university)大学

jiāo(to teach)教

Yīngyǔ(English)英语

tā(he,she,it)他,她,它

tāmen(they)他们

Měiguó(America)美国

rén(person,people)人

xué(to study)学

Additional Vocabulary

gōngzuò(work,job;to work)工作

lǎoshī(teacher)老师

xuéshēng(student)学生

nín(*formal form for "you"*)您

xìng(surname)姓

jiào(to be called)叫

míngzi(name,given name)名字

dà(big)大

xiǎo(small)小

zhōng(middle)中

xiānsheng(Mr.;husband)先生

tàitai(Mrs.;wife)太太

xiǎojiě(Miss;young woman)小姐

nǚshì(Ms.)女士

Useful Phrases

● Nǐ shì nǎ gè guójiā de rén?

(You are which country person?)

=What country are you from?

- Nǐ zài nǎli gōngzuò?

  (You at where work?)

  =Where do you work?

- Nǐ zuò shénme gōngzuò?

  (You do what work?)

  =What do you do?

- Wǒ shì lǎoshī.

  (I am a teacher.)

- Wǒ shì xuéshēng.

  (I am a student.)

- Qǐng wèn, nín guì xìng?

  (Please ask, your honorable name?)

  =May I ask your honorable surname?

This is a polite, formal way to ask someone's name. Appropriate especially for people whose social rank is higher than yours.

● Nǐ jiào shénme míngzi?

(You called what name?)

= What is your name?

This is less formal, more appropriate for social equals or children.

Forms of address:

xiānsheng (Mr.)

* Chén xiānsheng

= Mr. Chen.

Also means "husband."

tàitai (*Mrs.*)

* Chén tàitai

= Mrs. Chen.

Also means "wife" but sounds old-fashioned.

xiǎojiě (*Miss*)

* Chén xiǎojiě

= Miss Chen.

nǚshì (Ms.)

* Chén nǚshì

= Ms. Chen.

This is still relatively rare in China.

lǎoshī (*Teacher*)

* Chén lǎoshī

= Teacher Chen.

Note that these are added *<u>after</u>* *a person's family name.*

Sentence Patterns

How do I say "I am from (country)"?

Pattern: (who) + shì + cóng + (country) + lái + de.

Examples:

— Wǒ shì cóng Yīngguó lái de. (I am from England come's.) = I am from England.

— Wǒ shì cóng Rìběn lái de. (I am from Japan come's.) = I come from Japan.

— Wǒ shì cóng Měiguó lái de. (I am from America come's.) = I come from America.

The de *in this pattern is the same possessive* de *we have met previously.*

How do you say a person's nationality?

Pattern: (country name) + rén.

Examples:

— Měiguó rén = American.

— Jiānádà rén = Canadian.

What is the word order for saying where I do something?

Pattern: (Subject) + zài + (place) + (predicate).

Examples:

— Wǒ zài Nánjīng Dàxué jiāo Yīngyǔ. (I at Nanjing University teach English.)

— Wǒ zài Yīngguó gōngzuò. (I in England work.) = I work in England.

— Tā zài Jiānádà jiāo Hànyǔ. (He/she in Canada teaches Chinese.)

In Chinese word order, the place must come before the predicate. In other words, while in English you can say "I work in China," in Chinese you must say Wǒ zài Zhōngguó gōngzuò. *It is incorrect to say* * Wǒ gōngzuò zài Zhōngguó.

Notes

-men:

This suffix is added to form the plural of wǒ (I), nǐ (you), tā(he/she/it), and a few other words relating to people.

Nán Dà: = Nánjīng Dàxué = Nanjing University.

Names of schools are often abbreviated like this.

Practice Ideas

Practice with a tutor

***Reverse sentence drill*:**

To memorize a useful sentence that is a little long, start from the back. Examples:

jiāo Yīngyǔ.

zài Nánjīng Dàxué jiāo Yīngyǔ.

Wǒ zài Nánjīng Dàxué jiāo Yīngyǔ.

Ask your tutor to say the phrases, then you repeat. (This is also good tone practice.)

***Tone/Pinyin practice*:**

Bring a world map to class. On the map, point out a country and ask Zhè shì shénme guójiā? (This is what country?) As the tutor tells you, write down the name in *Pinyin*.

***Tone/Pinyin practice*:**

Ask your tutor for the names of one or two more

languages you are interested in. Note: Names of most languages are made with the word yǔ (language) as a suffix.

***Role play*:**

Do a role play based on the Dialogue above, one of you being the curious Chinese student and the other a foreigner looking to make friends.

***Map reading*:**

Using the Survival Characters, find as many of the locations as possible on a map of your city.

Practice on the street

***RLP*:**

Try to strike up a conversation at a store or somewhere else that will allow you to introduce yourself. (It is not at all uncommon for Chinese people to ask foreigners questions such as those in the Dialogue above.)

***Sign reading*:**

On a walk around the city, try to identify buildings

by reading the signs on them.

Extra Credit

Survival Characters

Using a city map, try to locate some of the following:

书店 shūdiàn (bookstore)　医院 yīyuàn (hospital)

银行 yínháng (bank)　大学 dàxué (university)

中学 zhōngxué (middle school)　小学 xiǎoxué (primary school)

博物馆 bówùguǎn (museum)　公园 gōngyuán (park)

Colloquial translation of Dialogue

A: Excuse me, which country are you from?

B: I'm from England.

A: What do you do in China?

B: I teach English at Nanjing University.

A: And them?

B: They are Americans. They study Chinese at Nanjing University.

Lesson 7: The Bookstore

In this lesson: "*I want to* ____." "*What kind of* ____?"

Signs: bookstore departments.

Core Lesson

Dialogue

B wants to make a purchase in a bookstore. A is the Chinese clerk.

A: Nǐ xiǎng mǎi shénme? (You want to buy what?)
你想买什么?

B: Wǒ xiǎng mǎi jǐ běn shū. (I want to buy several books.)
我想买几本书。

A：Shénmeyàng de shū?（What kind of books?）

什么样的书?

B：Yǒu méiyǒu Hànyǔ kèběn?（Have/not have Chinese textbooks?）

有没有汉语课本?

A：Méiyǒu. Nǐ hái yào shénme?（Not have. You still want what?）

没有。你还要什么?

B：Hàn-Yīng cídiǎn yǒu méiyǒu?（Chinese-English dictionary have or not?）

汉英词典有没有?

A：Yǒu. Hái yǒu ne?（Have. What else?）

有。还有呢?

B：Yī zhāng Běijīng shì dìtú.（One Beijing city map.）

一张北京市地图。

Dialogue Vocabulary

xiǎng(want to, *followed by verb*)想

běn(*measure word for books*)本

shénmeyàng de(what kind of)什么样的

kèběn(textbook)课本

hái(still, else)还

Hàn-Yīng(Chinese-English)汉英

cídiǎn(dictionary)词典

zhāng(*measure word for maps*)张

Běijīng shì(Beijing city)北京市

dìtú(map)地图

Additional Vocabulary

fàn(rice; food)饭

xǐ(to wash)洗

qù(to go)去

kàn(to look, read)看

yīfu(clothing)衣服

Useful Phrases

- Hái yǒu ne?

  (Still have?)

  = What else (would you like)?

Sentence Patterns

How do you say "I want (to do something)"?

Pattern: (subject) + xiǎng + (verb) + (object).

Examples:

— Wǒ xiǎng chī fàn. (I want to eat rice.) = I want to eat.

— Nǐ xiǎng kàn shū ma? (You want to read book?) = Do you want to read?

— Tā xiǎng xǐ yīfu. (He/she want to wash clothes.) = He/she wants to wash clothes.

— Wǒ xiǎng qù shūdiàn. (I want to go bookstore.) = I want to go to the bookstore.

How do you ask "Do you have ______?"

Chinese often uses a Topic-Comment sentence pattern, and this pattern can also be used to ask the "Do you have ______?" question.

Pattern: (topic) + yǒu méiyǒu?

Examples:

— Hàn-Yīng cídiǎn yǒu méiyǒu? (Chinese-English dictionary have/not have?)

— Hànyǔ kèběn yǒu méiyǒu? (Chinese textbook have/not have?)

Notes

***Chinese word order*:**

Chinese word order is sometimes flexible, especially

in spoken Chinese. Note that in the dialogue above, yǒu méiyǒu can come before the subject or after. Ex: Shū yǒu méiyǒu? (Books have not have?) and Yǒu méiyǒu shū? (Have not have books?) are both normal. In your own speaking you might initially choose to stick with one pattern, but expect to hear Chinese people vary the pattern.

***Chinese dictionaries*:**

When getting a dictionary for Chinese study, choose one with many example phrases and sentences so you can learn word usage as well as meaning. Examples also give you good clues as to connotations, level of formality, and so forth.

Practice Ideas

Practice with a tutor

***Review*:**

As fully as you can, introduce yourself to your tutor with an assumed identity. Feel free to make things up for practice and fun.

***Tone / Pinyin practice*:**

Ask your tutor how to say the names of several kinds of stores, using ______ zénme shuō? Then, as your tutor dictates the names, write them down in *Pinyin*. Variation: Ask about more items you want to buy.

***Usage*:**

There are several important new words in this lesson that are a little tricky to use: xiǎng (compared to yào), shénmeyàng de, hái, ne. Ask your tutor to give you some example sentences, or try making a few of your own.

***Role play*:**

Role play buying books in a bookstore. Use real books, dictionaries, maps and money; the realia almost inevitably forces you to experiment a little more.

Practice on the street

***RLP*:**

Shop for dictionaries, maps, and Chinese textbooks at a bookstore or bookstand.

***Field trip*:**

Have your tutor take you to nearby bookstores and show you what the different sections are and what is available there.

***Sign reading*:**

In a bookstore, try to locate various sections using the Survival Characters.

Extra Credit

Survival Characters

A bookstore may seem an intimidating place to practice reading Chinese, but knowing a few key characters can enable you to read quite a few signs there.

文学 wénxué(literature)

中国文学 zhōngguó wénxué(Chinese literature)

外国文学 wàiguó wénxué(foreign literature)

外文 wài wén (foreign language) *This marks the foreign language section of the store.*

文具 wénjù(culture tools) = stationery, pens, etc.

地图 dìtú(maps)

小说 xiǎoshuō(fiction)

Colloquial translation of Dialogue

A: What do you want to buy?

B: I want to buy several books.

A: What kind of books?

B: Do you have any Chinese textbooks?

A: No. What else do you want?

B: Do you have any Chinese-English dictionaries?

A: Yes. Anything else?

B: One Beijing city map.

Lesson 8: Getting Things Fixed

In this lesson: *Asking for help. Appliances, fixtures in rooms, apartments. Hot/cold. City maps: locating hotels.*

Core Lesson

Dialogue

Foreigner A needs help from Chinese guesthouse staff B. A's ability to explain is limited, so the goal is just to get someone to come and look.

A: Qǐng nǐ lái kànkan. (Please you come look look.)
请你来看看。

A：Cèsuǒ yǒu yīdiǎn wèntí.（Bathroom has a little problem.）

厕所有一点问题。

B：Shénme wèntí?（What problem?）

什么问题？

A：Mǎtǒng huài le.（Toilet has broken.）

马桶坏了。

A：Qǐng nǐ lái bāngmáng.（Please you come help.）

请你来帮忙。

Dialogue Vocabulary

kàn（to look）看

yīdiǎn（a little）一点

wèntí（problem; question）问题

mǎtǒng（toilet）马桶

huài（bad; to break）坏

le（*perfective marker — see "Notes"*）了

bāng（to help）帮

bāngmáng（to help）帮忙

Additional Vocabulary

rè（hot）热

lěng（cold）冷

kāi（to open）开

mén（door）门

kuài（fast）快

dǒng（to understand）懂

zhīdào(to know)知道

zài(again)再

shuō(to say, speak)说

cì(time, *as in "one time"*) 次

màn(slow)慢

xiūlǐ(to fix)修理

dōngxi(thing)东西

kōngtiáo(air conditioner) 空调

chuānghu(window)窗户

Useful Phrases

For problems in a room:

- Fángjiān tài rè/lěng.

  (Room too hot/cold.)

  =The room is too hot/cold.

- Qǐng (nǐ) bāng wǒ kāi mén.

  (Please you help me open door.)

  =Please open the door for me.

In older style Chinese guesthouses, often you are not given a key; a staff member is on duty to open your room door when you return.

- Qǐng nǐ kuài yīdiǎn.

  (Please you fast a little.)

  =Please hurry a little.

***For communication problems*:**

- Wǒ bù dǒng.

  (I don't understand.)

- Wǒ bù zhīdào.

  (I don't know.)

- Qǐng nǐ zài shuō yī cì.

  (Please you again say.)

  = Please say that again.

- Qǐng nǐ shuō màn yīdiǎn.

  (Please you speak slow a little.)

  = Please speak a little more slowly.

Sentence Patterns

How do I (politely) ask someone to do something for me?

Pattern: Qǐng + (nǐ) + bāng + (who) + (do what).

Examples:

— Qǐng bāng wǒ kāi mén. (Please help me open

door.) = Please open the door for me.

— Qǐng nǐ bāng wǒ xiūlǐ mǎtǒng. (Please you help me fix toilet.) = Please fix the toilet for me.

— Qǐng bāng tā mǎi yīdiǎn dōngxi. (Please help him/her buy a little things.) = Please buy a few things for him/her.

Notes

Kànkan:

This means "to take a look." In Chinese repeated verbs often have the sense of "a little" or "a bit." The following phrases have the same sense:

— kàn yī kàn (look one look) = take a look

— kàn yīxià (look one time) = take a look (See Lesson 10.)

Yǒu wèntí:

Literally wèntí means "problem" or "question," but in the phrase yǒu wèntí it often means "something wrong."

Examples:

— Tā yǒu wèntí. (He has problem.) = There's something wrong with him.

— Yǒu méiyǒu wèntí? (Have not have problem?) = Is everything okay? Any problems?

Le:

Whole dissertations have been written on this little word, but let's start with the simple idea that it indicates that an action has been completed.

Examples:

— Wǒ chī le. (I have eaten.) or (I ate.)

— Wǒ qù le. (I have gone.) or (I went.)

— Kōngtiáo huài le. (Air conditioning broke.) = The air conditioner has broken.

— Tā kāi le chuānghu. (He/she opened window.) = He/she opened the window.

Bāng *and* bāngmáng:

Both of these mean "to help," but bāng is followed by an object and bāngmáng is not.

Examples:

— Qǐng nǐ bāng wǒ. = Please help me. But:

— Qǐng nǐ bāngmáng. = Please help.

***Tip*: *The unfamiliarity of a new language*.**

One of the main problems Westerners face in studying Chinese is the sheer unfamiliarity of the language —it simply sounds so different from a Western language that initially it all seems a blur of sound. Do not despair. Slowly but surely your ears will get used to the sounds and contours of Chinese if you persist and give yourself time.

Practice Ideas

Practice with a tutor

***Review*:**

Practice making purchases at a bookstore.

***Tones / Pinyin / vocabulary*:**

In your apartment (hotel room, guesthouse room, etc.) point to equipment and appliances (especially those that might break or have already caused problems) and ask your tutor to say the names of the objects in Chinese as you write them down in *Pinyin*. Keep a notebook.

***Usage*:**

Practice making sentences using le, bāng, and bāngmáng.

***Role play*:**

Get someone to come to help with a problem in your room. Explain what you can about the problem.

***Map reading*:**

Using the Survival Characters as clues, try to find hotels, etc. on a city map.

Practice on the street

***RLP*:**

If there are any problems in your room, try to explain the problem to staff yourself before calling for an interpreter.

***Sign reading*:**

Out on the street, try to identify hotels, etc. by

reading their Chinese signs.

***Map reading*:**

Use your map to guide you to a nearby hotel.

Extra Credit

Survival Characters

Being able to locate hotels and guesthouses on maps is useful not only if you are looking for a place to stay, but also if you are looking for Western restaurants and products — large hotels serving an international clientele are often one of the best places to look. The characters below are often found in the names of hotels.

宾馆 bīnguǎn(hotel)

饭店 fàndiàn(restaurant) Often used in the names of large hotels.

酒店 jiǔdiàn(restaurant) Also often part of hotel names. (Literally means "wine shop.")

招待所 zhāodàisuǒ (guesthouse) A guesthouse is generally more modest than a hotel.

Extra Credit Vocabulary

***Electric Appliances*:**

Chinese names of these often include the word diàn (electric).

电视 diànshì(electric look) = television
电灯 diàndēng(electric lamp) = light
电话 diànhuà(electric speech) = telephone

Colloquial translation of Dialogue

A: Please come and take a look. There's something wrong with the bathroom.

B: What's the problem?

A: The toilet is broken. Please come and help.

Lesson 9: Drinks And Snacks

In this lesson: "*I'm hungry/thirsty.*" *Containers for beverages.* "*A sweet one.*" *Either/or questions. Signs: snackshop freezers.*

Core Lesson

Dialogue

A and B are hungry/thirsty foreigners passing a local general store.

A: Wǒ è le. Nǐ ne? (I hungry. You?)
我饿了。你呢?

B: Wǒ bú è, dànshì yǒu yīdiǎn kě. (I not hungry, but a little thirsty.)

我不饿，但是有一点渴。

(*They go over to the general store to see what is on offer. C is the Chinese proprietor.*)

A：Nǐ yǒu méiyǒu bǐnggān?（You have not have cookies?）

你有没有饼干？

C：Yǒu. Nǐ yào nǎ zhǒng?（Have. You want which kind?）

有。你要哪种？

A：(*Pointing*) Zhè zhǒng shì tián de hái shì xián de? (This kind is sweet or salty?)

这种是甜的还是咸的？

C：Zhè zhǒng shì qiǎokèlì de.（This kind is chocolate.）

这种是巧克力的。

B：(*While A ponders.*) Wǒ yào yī gè kělè. (I want a cola.)

我要一个可乐。

C：Dà píng hái shì xiǎo píng?（Big bottle or little bottle?）

大瓶还是小瓶？

B：Wǒ yào guàn zhuāng de. (I want can filled.)

我要罐装的。

Dialogue Vocabulary

è(hungry)饿
kě(thirsty)渴
bǐnggān(crackers, cookies) 饼干
zhǒng(kind, type)种
hái shì(or)还是
tián(sweet)甜
xián(salty)咸
qiǎokèlì(chocolate)巧克力
kělè(cola)可乐
píng (*measure word*; bottle)瓶
guàn(can)罐
zhuāng(to fill; to install) 装

Additional Vocabulary

suān(sour)酸
là(hot)辣
bīngqílín(ice cream)冰淇淋
gān(dry)干
hē(to drink)喝
miànbāo(bread)面包
bēizi(cup)杯子
píngzi(bottle)瓶子
guàntou(can)罐头

***Beverages*:**

qìshuǐ(soda pop)汽水
kāfēi(coffee)咖啡
chá(tea)茶
shuǐ(water)水

kāishuǐ(boiled water)开水

bīng shuǐ(ice water)冰水

píjiǔ(beer)啤酒

pútaojiǔ(wine)葡萄酒

báijiǔ(hard Chinese liquor)白酒

guǒzhī(fruit juice)果汁

niúnǎi(milk)牛奶

kuàngquánshuǐ (mineral water)矿泉水

***Measure words for beverages*:**

From the word:

bēi(a cup of)杯

píng(a bottle of)瓶

guàn(a can of)罐

bāo(a package of;a package)包

Examples:

yī bēi shuǐ = a cup of water

yī píng qìshuǐ = a bottle of soda pop

yī guàn kělè = a can of cola

yī bāo bǐnggān = a package of cookies/crackers

Sentence Patterns

How do I say "I'm a bit hungry"?

Pattern: (subject) + yǒu yīdiǎn + (adjective).

Examples:

— Wǒ yǒu yīdiǎn è. (I have a bit hungry.) = I'm a bit hungry.

— Wǒ yǒu yīdiǎn rè. (I have a little hot.) = I'm a little hot.

— Zhèr yǒu yīdiǎn lěng. (Here has a little cold.) = It's a little cold here.

How do I say "a sweet one (a big one, etc.)"?

Pattern: (adjective) + de.

Examples:

— Wǒ yào nà gè dà de. (I want that big one.) = I want that big one (rather than another one).

— Tā xiǎng mǎi xián de. (He/she wants to buy salty.) = He/she wants to buy the salty kind (not the sweet kind).

— Wǒ xiǎng chī là de. (I want to eat spicy hot one.) = I want to eat something spicy hot (rather than something else).

How do I ask an either/or question?

Pattern: (A) + hái shì + (B).

Examples:

- ***For adjectives*:**

— Zhè shì suān de hái shì là de? (This is sour or hot?) = Is this sour or hot?

— Nǐ yào dà de hái shì xiǎo de? (You want big or small?) = Do you want a big one or a small one?

- ***For nouns*:**

— Nǐ xiǎng chī miànbāo hái shì bǐnggān? (You want to eat bread or crackers?) = Do you want to eat bread or crackers?

Notes

Bǐnggān:

This word can mean either (sweet) cookies or (salty) crackers. Hence the need for A's question in the Dialogue above.

Tip: Finding time.

One of the greatest problems that learners outside formal language study programs face is a shortage of time — and usually an abundance of other things that need to be done. Usually in order to sustain even a modest study program, you need to regularly block out a portion of prime time in your daily schedule (i. e. time when you are reasonably alert) that can be devoted to Chinese study, and generally this means making sacrifices in some other area of your life. Attempts to learn a language without allocating adequate time to the task usually result in more frustration than progress. In contrast, even if you can only find half an hour of quality time each day for Chinese study, you will be able to make gradual but genuine progress.

Practice Ideas

Practice with a tutor

***Review*:**

Practice getting help when your toilet clogs or something else is broken.

***Vocabulary + tone/Pinyin practice*:**

Have your tutor recommend several Chinese snack foods to you by dictating the names.

***Usage*:**

Practice making sentences with hái shì.

***Role play*:**

Role play buying drinks and snacks at a store or a restaurant.

***Menu reading*:**

Ask your tutor to copy down a simple Chinese menu from a refreshment stand (the kind of menu that is often written on a blackboard). Then work with the tutor to see how much of it you can decipher. You may only know a few characters, but insist that the tutor let you try to figure it out first.

Practice on the street

***RLP*:**

Buy some drinks and snacks at a local store or refreshment stand.

***Field trip*:**

Ask your tutor or a Chinese friend to take you to a store and show you some of the snack foods he/she enjoys and would recommend to you.

Extra Credit

Survival Characters

Little roadside stands in China often have coolers with drinks and cold snacks inside, and the contents of the cooler are often written on a poster or chalkboard. The next time you pass such a stand, see if you can spot any of the following characters:

水 shuǐ (water). This is found in kuàngquán shuǐ (mineral water).

冰 bīng (ice, cold). This is found in bīngqílín (ice cream).

雪 xuě (snow). This is found in the names of various ice creams and drinks.

Colloquial translation of the Dialogue

A: I'm hungry. How about you?

B: I'm not hungry, but I'm a little thirsty.

....

A: Do you have any cookies?

C: Yes. What kind do you want?

A: (Pointing) Is this kind sweet or salty?

C: This kind is chocolate.

B: (While A ponders) I want a cola.

C: Big or small bottle?

B: I want a can.

Lesson 10: The Noodle Stand

In this lesson: *Ordering noodles, etc. "Do you like ____?" Menus: noodle stands.*

Core Lesson

Dialogue

Foreigner B is ordering a meal at a small Chinese noodle stand. A is the Chinese proprietor.

A: Nǐ xiǎng chī shénme? (You want to eat what?)

你想吃什么?

B: Děng yīxià. (Wait a minute.)

等一下。

B：Wǒ kàn yīxià càidān.（I look a moment menu.）

我看一下菜单。

………………

B：Hǎo. Wǒ lái yī wǎn miàntiáo.（Okay. I take one bowl noodles.）

好。我来一碗面条。

A：Hǎo. Nǐ hái yào chī shénme?（Okay. You else want to eat what?）

好。你还要吃什么？

A：Nǐ xǐhuān chī jiǎozi ma?（You like to eat jiǎozi?）

你喜欢吃饺子吗？

B：Hěn xǐhuān. Wǒ yě yào yī dié jiǎozi.（Very much like. I also want one plate jiǎozi.）

很喜欢。我也要一碟饺子。

Dialogue Vocabulary

děng（to wait）等

yīxià（a moment）一下

càidān（menu）菜单

lái（to come；to take）来

wǎn（bowl；a bowl of）碗

miàntiáo（noodles）面条

xǐhuān（to like）喜欢

yě（also）也

jiǎozi（pork/vegetable dumpling）饺子

dié（plate；a plate of）碟

Additional Vocabulary

huì(can; able to)会　　yòng(to use)用

kuàizi(chopsticks)筷子　　cài(dishes, food)菜

jié zhàng(to count up a bill)结账　　zǒu(to walk; to leave)走

Useful Phrases

- Qǐng jié zhàng.

  (Please count up bill.)

  = Please get me the bill.

"Jié zhàng" *is sufficient, but more abrupt.*

Questions you will often hear in restaurants:

- Nǐ huì bú huì yòng kuàizi?

  (You can cannot use chopsticks?)

  = Can you use chopsticks?

- Nǐ xǐhuān Zhōngguó cài ma?

  (You like Chinese dishes?)

  = Do you like Chinese food?

Sentence Patterns

How do I say "wait a minute (a bit, etc.)"?

Many verbs involving a sense of duration can be followed by yīxià (a moment, a minute, a bit).

Pattern: (verb) + yīxià.

Examples:

— děng yīxià = wait a minute

— kàn yīxià = look for a minute

— zǒu yīxià = walk a bit

How do I place an order at a restaurant?

The word lái (to come; to take) is often used in placing orders at a restaurant.

Pattern: (Subject) + lái + (amount) + (measure word) + (item).

Examples:

— Wǒ lái yīdiǎn jī. (I take a little chicken.) = I'll take some chicken.

— Wǒmen lái liǎng wǎn miàn. (We take two bowl noodles.) = We'll take two bowls of noodles.

— Wǒ lái sān gè bāozi. (I take three *baozi*.) = I'll

take three *baozi* .

Notes

Hěn xǐhuān:

Note the word order in the phrase hěn xǐhuān(very like) = like very much. The hěn (very) comes before xǐhuān(like), unlike word order in English.

Tip : Accents and dialects .

One frustration of learning Chinese from average people instead of language teachers is that not all Chinese use standard Chinese pronunciation. In fact, there are only a few places in China (such as Changchun, but definitely not Beijing) where the average person actually pronounces things the way textbooks say they should. Furthermore, in many provinces Chinese people speak a dialect and only learn Putonghua as a second language.

First, accept this as a reality rather than burning a lot of emotional energy getting frustrated by it. Perhaps even revel in it as a reflection of China's rich regional diversity. Second, get used to guessing; that sentence that sounded vaguely like Ni hao! might actually have been Ni hɑo, albeit with a heavy local accent. Third, learn a few words in the local dialect. You will probably get all kinds of brownie points with local people for knowing a few of their words.

Practice Ideas

Practice with a tutor

***Review*:**

Practice getting something to drink at a refreshment stand.

***Vocabulary + tone/Pinyin practice*:**

Have your tutor dictate a list of foods to you, some from this lesson and some that are new to you.

***Usage*:**

Practice making sentences with xǐhuān and yīxià.

***Role play*:**

Role play ordering a meal at a noodle stand. Ask what they have and how much things cost, then tell the proprietor what you like/want. Compliment the cook on the food after the meal.

***Menu reading*:**

Ask your tutor to copy down a simple Chinese menu from a local noodle stand or student dining hall. Then work with the tutor to see how much of it you can decipher. You may only know a few characters, but insist that the tutor let you try to figure it out first.

Practice on the street

***RLP*:**

Order a meal at a local eatery. For smaller noodle stands the menu may be scrawled on a blackboard, or there may be no menu at all — they may just concoct what you ask for with whatever is on hand. If it is a nice restaurant with a printed menu, spend some time thumbing through the menu. Noodles, fried rice, and so forth are usually near the end of the menu.

***Field trip*:**

Ask your tutor or another Chinese friend to take

you to look at a few small Chinese restaurants and show you how to order a meal there.

Extra Credit

You may want to learn at least a few of these characters so you can begin reading menus, especially the simple kind written on noodle stand signs. Despite the fact that Chinese people often consider items like those below as xiǎo chī (little eats = snacks) more than a proper meal, they are generally a foreigner's best first bet for successfully ordering a filling meal at a Chinese noodle shop or roadside food stall.

Extra Credit Vocabulary

miàntiáo(noodles)面条
chǎo fàn(fried rice)炒饭
mántou(steamed bread)馒头
bāozi(steamed bread with filling)包子
jiān bǐng(fried flat bread)煎饼
shāo bǐng(baked flat bread)烧饼
jiǎozi(see above)饺子
yóutiáo(deep fried bread sticks)油条

Colloquial translation of Dialogue

A : What do you want to eat?

B : Wait a minute. I'll take a look at the menu.

....

B : Okay(I'm ready). I'll take a bowl of noodles.

A : Okay. What else do you want to have? Do you like *jiaozi*?

B : Yes, I like *jiaozi* a lot. I also want one plate of *jiaozi*.

Lesson 11: Buying (III)

In this lesson: *Colors. Sizes. Making polite requests. Clothing. City maps: stores.*

Core Lesson

Dialogue

In some Chinese shops goods are behind a counter and you have to ask a clerk to get the item for you. A is attempting to make a rather mundane purchase in such a shop.

A: Nǐmen zhèr yǒu méiyǒu máojīn? (You here have not have towels?)

你们这儿有没有毛巾？

B: Yǒu. Nǐ yào shénme yánsè? (Have. You want

what color?)

有。你要什么颜色?

A: Wǒ yào hóngsè de. (I want a red-colored one.)

我要红色的。

B: Wǒmen yǒu dà de, xiǎo de. (We have big ones, small ones.)

我们有大的,小的。

B: Nǐ yào shénmeyàng de? (You want what kind?)

你要什么样的?

A: Máfan nǐ gěi wǒ kàn nà gè dà de. (Trouble you give me look at that big one.)

麻烦你给我看那个大的。

B: Nǎ gè? (Which one?)(While searching.)

哪个?

A: Duì! Nà gè! (Right! That!)

对! 那个!

Dialogue Vocabulary

zhèr(here)这儿 máojīn(towel)毛巾

yánsè(color)颜色 hóngsè(red)红色

dà(big)大 shénmeyàng(what kind) 什么样

xiǎo(small)小

máfan(trouble; to trouble)麻烦

duì(correct, right)对

gěi(give)给

nà gè(that)那个

Additional Vocabulary

***Colors*:**

hēi(black)黑

bái(white)白

huáng(yellow)黄

lán(blue)蓝

lǜ(green)绿

huī(gray)灰

Useful Phrases

- Hǎo kàn.

  (Good looking)

  = Looks nice.

Used for clothing, objects, even people.

Sentence Patterns

How can I politely make a request?

Pattern: Máfan nǐ + (request).

Examples:

— Máfan nǐ gěi wǒ nà gè máojīn. (Bother you give

me that towel.) = May I bother you to give me that towel?

— Máfan nǐ kāi mén. (Bother you to open door.) = Can I trouble you to open the door?

— Máfan nǐ gěi wǒ kàn nà gè dōngxi. (Bother you let me look at that thing.) = Would you give me a look at that thing?

How do I say what color (of something) I want?

Pattern: (color) + de. Or (color) + sè + de.

Examples:

— Wǒ yào nà gè hóng de. (I want that red one.)

— Wǒ xiǎng mǎi nà gè bái sè de. (I want to buy that white colored one.)

The sè *in this pattern is optional.*

Notes

Máfan:

Máfan also means "trouble" as in hěn máfan (a lot of trouble).

Measure words:

A reminder that if you can't remember the correct

measure word, you can often get away with using gè. For example, the proper measure word for máojīn (towel) is tiáo, but gè is a passable substitute.

-er *endings*:

In northern China, an -er ending is added to many words. For example, while southern Chinese would say zhèlǐ(here), northerners would say zhèr. You need to decide if you want to follow northern or southern custom (or learn to switch depending on your audience), but for now focus on not getting confused too much by these regional variations when you listen.

Tips: Tones.

At the early stages of Chinese study and use you may make quite a few tone mistakes when you speak. Generally a tone mistake in the context of a sentence won't confuse a Chinese person too much, but if you speak in isolated words and get the tones wrong, Chinese may not understand you. So one strategy for minimizing tones as a communication problem is to create context by using complete phrases or sentences — or lots of body language.

Practice Ideas

Practice with a tutor

***Review*:**

Role play ordering a meal in a noodle stand.

***Tone/Pinyin practice*:**

Point to various colors or items of clothing and have your tutor pronounce them while you write the words down in your notebook.

***Usage*:**

Practice making sentences relating to clothing and colors.

***Role play*:**

Role play buying clothes in a store where things are behind a counter and you have to tell the clerk what size, color, or item you want.

***Map reading*:**

Using the Survival Characters, locate different

kinds of stores on a city map.

Practice on the street

***RLP*:**

Go to a store and try to buy a towel or some other object that is behind a counter. Try to use your Chinese as well as pointing.

***Field trip*:**

Ask a Chinese friend to take you clothes shopping.

Extra Credit

Survival Characters

Locate some of the following on your city map. They may appear either independently or as part of the name of a building.

商场 shāngchǎng(a mall, a gathering of shops)
公司 gōngsī(company)
大厦 dà shà (building, usually a large commercial

building)
百货公司 bǎihuò gōngsī(department store)
百货大楼 bǎihuò dàlóu(department store)

Extra Credit Vocabulary

***Clothing*:**

chènshān(shirt, blouse)衬衫
máoyī(sweater)毛衣
qúnzi(skirt)裙子
kùzi(pants)裤子
wàitào(coat)外套
nèiyī(underwear)内衣
xiézi(shoes)鞋子
wàzi(socks)袜子
tuōxié(thongs)拖鞋

***Other clothing related words*:**

xīn(new)新
jiù(old)旧
cháng(long)长
duǎn(short)短
kuān(wide, broad)宽
zhǎi(narrow)窄
shēn(deep)深
Can be used for colors. Ex:
shēn lánsè = deep blue
qiǎn(shallow)浅
Can be used for colors. Ex:
qiǎn lánsè = light blue

Colloquial translation of Dialogue

A: Do you have any towels here?

B: Yes. What color do you want?

A: I want red.

B: We have big ones and little ones. What kind do you want?

A: Could you let me have a look at that big one?

B: (While searching) Which one?

A: Yeah, that one!

Lesson 12: Asking The Time

In this lesson: *Time. "How long ____?" Present continuous tense ("I am ____ ing.") Day, month, year. Calendar characters.*

Core Lesson

Dialogue

Chinese person A accosts Chinese-looking foreigner B to ask the time, and quickly discovers B isn't Chinese.

A: Qǐng wèn, xiànzài jǐdiǎn le? (May I ask, now what time?)

请问,现在几点了?

B: Sān diǎn wǔshí fēn. (Three o'clock fifty minutes.)

三点五十分。

A：Nǐ shì xuéshēng ma?（You are student?）

你是学生吗？

B：Bú shì, wǒ shì Rìyǔ lǎoshī.（No, I am Japanese language teacher.）

不是，我是日语老师。

B：Dànshì, wǒ yě zài xuéxí Hànyǔ.（But, I also am learning Chinese.）

但是，我也在学习汉语。

A：Nǐ yǐjīng xué le duōjiǔ?（You already have studied how long?）

你已经学了多久？

B：Jǐ gè yuè.（A few months.）

几个月。

A：Nǐ jìnbù hěn kuài.（You progress very fast.）

你进步很快。

B：Nǎli, nǎli.（Where, where.）

哪里，哪里。

Dialogue Vocabulary

xiànzài（now）现在　　jǐdiǎn（what time）几点

diǎn（o'clock）点　　fēn（minute; minutes）分

Rìyǔ(Japanese language) 日语

xuéxí(to study)学习

jìnbù(progress; to progress) 进步

dànshì(but, however)但是

yǐjīng(already)已经

duōjiǔ(how long)多久

yuè(month; months)月

Additional Vocabulary

tiān (day)天

zuò (to do)做

zhōng (clock)钟

jīntiān (today)今天

míngtiān (tomorrow)明天

nián (year)年

xíguàn (to be accustomed to)习惯

zuótiān (yesterday)昨天

hòutiān (day after tomorrow)后天

***Days of the week*:**

Names for the days of the week are formed using the pattern xīngqī (or lǐbài) + number. (Note that "Sunday" is an exception.)

xīngqī yī (Monday)

xīngqī'èr (Tuesday)

xīngqī sān (Wednesday)

xīngqī sì (Thursday)

xīngqī wǔ (Friday)

xīngqī liù (Saturday)

xīngqī tiān (Sunday) (*Also* xīngqī rì)

For all of the above, lǐbài *can be substituted for* xīngqī.

Months:

For months of the year, the pattern is: (number) + yuè.

yī yuè (January)	èr yuè (February)
sān yuè(March)	sì yuè (April)
wǔ yuè (May)	liù yuè (June)
qī yuè (July)	bā yuè (August)
jiǔ yuè (September)	shí yuè (October)
shíyī yuè (November)	shí'èr yuè (December)

Note the difference between:

— yī gè yuè = one month

— yī yuè = January

Years:

To indicate years, the pattern is: (number) + nián.

Examples:

— Yī jiǔ bā sān nián. (One nine eight three year.) = 1983.

— Liǎng qiān nián. (Two thousand year.) = 2000.

Useful Phrases

- Nǐ zài Zhōngguó xíguàn ma?

  (You in China accustomed?)

  = Are you used to life in China?

This is a question you will often be asked.

Sentence Patterns

***How do I state a time*?**

For telling the hour:

Pattern: (number) + diǎn (zhōng).

Adding zhōng "*clock*" *after* diǎn *is optional in this pattern.*)

Examples:

— liǎng diǎn = two o'clock

— sì diǎn zhōng = four o'clock

For telling minutes:

Pattern: (number) + fēn.

Examples:

— liǎng diǎn shí fēn = 2:10

— bā diǎn sānshísān fēn = 8:33

How do I say "I am (doing something)"?

Pattern: zài + (verb).

Examples:

— Wǒ zài chī fàn. (I am eating.)

— Tā zài mǎi shū. (He/she is buying books.)

What is the word order for using yǐjīng **(already) in a sentence?**

Pattern: (subject) + yǐjīng + (predicate).

Examples:

— Tā yǐjīng zài Zhōngguó liǎng nián. (He already in China two years.)

— Nǐ yǐjīng zài cèsuǒ hěn jiǔ. (You already in bathroom very long.) = You have already been in the bathroom a long time!

Notice that, unlike "already" in English, yǐjīng *can't be placed at the end of a sentence.*

How do I answer "how long" questions?

Below are sample answer patterns for "how long" questions like Nǐ yǐjīng zài Zhōngguó duō jiǔ? (*How long have you already been in China?*)

— Yī fēn zhōng. (One minute.)

For this pattern, you must add zhōng.

— Yī gè xiǎoshí. (One hour.)

Also: Yī gè zhōngtóu.

— Yī tiān. (One day.)

— Yī gè xīngqī. (One week.)

— Yī gè yuè. (One month.)

— Yī nián. (One year.)

Note which of the above require a measure word and which do not.

Notes

Tip: *Morale in language learning*.

Sometimes learning Chinese can seem hopeless; there is so much to learn and your progress seems so slow. This is less of a problem during the first few exciting days of Chinese study than later as Chinese study becomes less fresh and new, but even early on it can be a problem.

To keep yourself going, it helps to take things one step at a time rather than brooding over how far away the goal of total mastery is. Set a series of limited and reasonable goals for yourself, and then keep putting one foot in front of the other until you achieve them. Every time you reach a little goal, reward yourself with a pat on the back, a chocolate bar, and a satisfied look back at what you have already learned. Success in language learning has more to do with persistence in making small steps than it does with any magical "gift for languages."

Practice Ideas

Practice with a tutor

***Review*:**

Role play buying things at a store. Be particular about colors and sizes.

***Speaking/listening practice*:**

Bring some pictures to a class of people involved in a variety of activities. Then, using the Tā zài + (verb) pattern, tell your tutor what the people in the pictures are doing. If you need help, point and ask Tā zài zuò shénme? (She/he is doing what?)

***Listening practice*:**

Have your tutor dictate times (days, months, years) in Chinese while you write them down.

***Usage*:**

Practice giving the time.

***Usage*:**

Make sentences involving days and dates. (It may help if you have a calendar handy.)

***Role play*:**

Do a role play following the dialogue above. Be sure to compliment your tutor on something and note not only what he/she says but also any body language.

***Reading*:**

Find a hotel registration form or something similar and, using the Survival Chinese characters below, go over it with your tutor to see how much you can make out.

Practice on the street

***RLP*:**

At a store, at the front desk of the guesthouse, or wherever, ask some Chinese person the time. Follow up with conversation as possible.

Extra Credit

Survival Characters

You will see these characters on calendars and many kinds of forms, for example, the kind you need to fill out in hotels.

日 rì(day)
月 yuè(month)
年 nián(year)
姓 xìng(family name)
名 míng(given name)
出生日 chū shēng rì(born day) = date of birth

Colloquial translation of Dialogue

A: Excuse me, what time is it now?

B: 3:50.

A: Are you a student?

B: No, I'm a Japanese teacher. But I am also studying Chinese.

A: How long have you already studied?

B: A few months.

A: Your progress is fast.

B: No, not really.

Lesson 13: The Restaurant

In this lesson: *Ordering in a restaurant. Foods. Making suggestions. Menus: dishes.*

Core Lesson

Dialogue

Foreigner B and friend have been emboldened by earlier success with noodles to try ordering a more sophisticated meal at a local restaurant. A is the eager waitress.

A: Nǐmen chī shénme cài? (You eat what dishes?)
你们吃什么菜?

B: Yǒu shénme hǎo chī de? (Have what good to eat?)

有什么好吃的？

A：Xiā，xíng bù xíng？（Shrimp，okay？）

虾，行不行？

B：Qǐng nǐ gěi wǒ kàn kan càidān.（Please you give me look at menu.）

请你给我看看菜单。

（*A cooperatively pulls out a menu and points.*）

B：Xiā bǐjiào guì. Hái yǒu biéde ma？（Shrimp rather expensive. Also have other？）

虾比较贵。还有别的吗？

A：Qīngjiāo ròupiàn，zěnmeyàng？（Green pepper with pork slices，what about it？）

青椒肉片，怎么样？

B：Hǎo. Wǒmen zài lái yī gè qīng cài…（OK. We also want a green vegetable dish…）

好。我们再来一个青菜……

B：…yī wǎn suān là tāng…（... a bowl of hot-sour soup...）

……一碗酸辣汤……

B：…liǎng wǎn mǐ fàn.（... two bowls of rice.）

……两碗米饭。

Dialogue Vocabulary

cài (vegetable; generic term for meat/vegetable dishes)菜

xiā (shrimp)虾

bǐjiào (comparatively; rather)比较

qīngjiāo(green pepper)青椒

zěnmeyàng (how about)怎么样

suān là (sour-hot)酸辣

mǐ fàn (cooked rice)米饭

xíng (okay)行

biéde(other)别的

ròupiàn (pork slices)肉片

qīng cài (leafy green vegetable)青菜

tāng (soup)汤

Additional Vocabulary

wèijīng (MSG)味精

bǎo (full)饱

gòu (enough)够

gān (dry; to dry)干

zìjǐ (self)自己

Useful Phrases

● Bù yào wèijīng, hǎo bù hǎo?

(Don't want MSG, okay?)

= No MSG, okay?

***Useful banquet phrases*:**

- Gān bēi!

  (Dry glass!)

  = Bottoms up!

Frequently heard at banquets, this means to drink your glass dry.

- Wǒ chī bǎo le.

  (I have eaten full.)

  = I'm full.

Useful for explaining why you can't eat any more.

- Wǒ zìjǐ lái.

  (I myself do.)

  = I can do it myself.

Useful when a host insists on putting food in your bowl for you—perhaps things you don't want.

- Gòu le!

  (Enough!)

Useful when a zealous host heaps too much food in your bowl.

Sentence Patterns

How do I make a suggestion?

One pattern for making suggestions is: (noun phrase/sentence) + zěnmeyàng?

Examples:

— Miàntiáo zěnmeyàng? (Noodles, how about?) = How about having noodles?

— Chī xiā zěnmeyàng? (Eat shrimp, how about?) = How about eating shrimp?

Also:

Nǐ zěnmeyàng? = How are you doing? or Are you okay?

Notes

Mǐ fàn:

Fàn means both "rice" and "food" in general. Mǐ fàn is more specific, meaning only "cooked rice." By itself the word mǐ means "uncooked rice", and if you go to buy a bag of rice you need to ask for mǐ.

Qīng cài:

In some parts of China this is what they call the local green leafy vegetable; in other areas there are a variety of such vegetables and qīng cài is a generic term. In the latter areas if you ask for qīng cài in a restaurant they may ask what kind you want. (It is pretty safe to just order one at random — they are generally all fairly inexpensive, healthy, and good.)

***Strategy*: *Ordering in a restaurant*.**

If you know what you want — and how to say what you want — there is no problem. However, often this is not the case, so the Dialogue above models a coping strategy. Ask the staff to recommend something, but most places will recommend their best — and most expensive — so check what they recommend on the menu to ensure that it isn't beyond your means. Tip: Ask before ordering a dish that has no price listed next to it — these are usually the expensive delicacies.

***Tip*: *Memorizing vocabulary*.**

Learning a new language requires memorizing lots of vocabulary (as this lesson clearly demonstrates), so you need to develop good strategies for embedding lots of new words in your memory. Some suggestions:

1) Repetition: The more times you see (hear, say, write) a word, the more likely you are to remember it.

2) Concentration: Staying alert when you memorize is vitally important.

3) Application: A word that you find a chance to use in a conversation is more likely to stay with you than one you only study in a book.

4) Movement: Physical movement combined with memorization helps you remember words better. Sway your arms, rock your head, pace the room, do whatever you need to.

5) Associations: Associate a word with something that is memorable, funny, shocking, etc. It may help to associate the Chinese word with some word in your own language that the Chinese word sounds like — the more absurd, the better.

Practice Ideas

Practice with a tutor

***Review*:**

Practice time, days of the week, and answers to "how long" questions.

***Tones / Pinyin / vocabulary practice*:**

Ask your tutor to recommend some good Chinese dishes to you, dictating the names in Chinese.

***Usage*:**

Practice making sentences with zěnmeyàng.

***Role play*:**

Order a meal in a restaurant. Do this several times, switching roles.

***Menu reading*:**

Learn the names of some Chinese dishes (see below), and then check the menu at the end of this lesson to see if you can spot your dishes in an all-Chinese menu.

Practice on the street

***RLP*:**

Go out to have a meal and use as much Chinese as you can in the process. (If you go in a group, agree that as much of the ordering as possible will be done by those who know the least Chinese — others can help.)

***RLP*:**

Ask a Chinese person (guesthouse staff? a bored store clerk?) about good Chinese foods you should try. In your notebook write down one or two that sound promising so you can ask your tutor about them.

***Menu hunt*:**

Locate a real restaurant menu and copy it for study use.

Extra Credit

Survival Characters

Chinese restaurant menus usually organize food by category. Meat dishes usually appear up front, often divided into beef, pork, chicken, fish, and/or seafood. Next comes a vegetable section (tofu dishes are generally here), and finally the noodle and other carbohydrate items come at the end. You have already encountered most of the characters which mark these sections, but for good measure here they are again:

肉 ròu (meat; often pork) 牛肉 niú ròu (beef)

猪肉 zhū ròu (pork) 鸡肉 jī ròu (chicken)

鱼 yú (fish) 海鲜 hǎixiān (seafood)

蔬菜 shūcài (vegetables) 面食 miànshí (noodles, etc.)

Extra Credit Vocabulary

mǐ (uncooked rice)米

tiáogēng (spoon)调羹

tāngchí (spoon; soup spoon)汤匙

sháozi (ladle)勺子

jiàngyóu (soy sauce)酱油

yóu (oil)油	wèijīng (MSG)味精
cù (vinegar)醋	yán (salt)盐
làjiāo jiàng (hot sauce)辣椒酱	táng (sugar)糖
	suàn (garlic)蒜

Some Chinese dishes beloved by foreigners:

dàn huā tāng (egg flower soup)蛋花汤

suān là tāng (sour-hot soup)酸辣汤

mápó dòufu (spicy bean curd)麻婆豆腐

yú xiāng ròu sī (spicy pork threads)鱼香肉丝

yú xiāng qiézi (spicy eggplant)鱼香茄子

táng cù lǐ ji (sweet sour pork)糖醋里脊

jiācháng dòufu (homestyle tofu)家常豆腐

gōngbào jīdīng (princess chicken)宫爆鸡丁

yāoguǒ jīdīng (cashew chicken)腰果鸡丁

hóng shāo niú ròu (braised beef)红烧牛肉

xīhóngshì chǎo dàn (tomato scrambled eggs)西红柿炒蛋

kǔguā chǎo dàn (bitter melon scrambled eggs)苦瓜炒蛋

chǎo qīng cài (fried green vegetables)炒青菜

sì jì dòu (four season beans)四季豆

kōng xīn cài ("empty heart" vegetable)空心菜

zhá tǔdòu tiáo (fried potato threads)炸土豆条

bá sī xiāngjiāo (candied bananas)拔丝香蕉

Colloquial translation of Dialogue

A: What (dishes) would you like to eat?

B: What's good?

A: How about shrimp?

B: Please let me look at the menu.

(A cooperatively pulls out menu and points.)

B: Shrimp is a bit expensive. Do you have anything else?

A: How about green pepper with pork slices?

B: Okay. We'll also take a green vegetable dish, a bowl of hot-sour soup, and two bowls of rice.

A Chinese Menu[1]

1. 汤类

酸辣汤	4.00	杏仁鸡蛋汤	5.00
鱼头汤	10.00	蛋花汤	4.00

2. 肉类

糖醋里脊	12.00	炒腊肠	10.00
红烧猪肉	12.00	鱼香肉丝	12.00

3. 鸡类

辣子鸡	12.00	蘑菇粉皮鸡	15.00
宫爆鸡丁	8.00	腰果鸡丁	8.00

1 This is a shortened version of a menu procured by Holly Herrin from a little restaurant in Tai'an, Shandong.

4. 蔬菜

青椒炒肉	6.00	芹菜炒肉	4.00
红烧茄子	6.00	红烧豆腐	5.00
清炒小白菜	3.00	西红柿炒鸡蛋	6.00
清炒土豆丝	3.00	麻婆豆腐	5.00
炸土豆条	4.00	空心菜	4.00
四季豆炒胡萝卜	4.00	拔丝苹果	6.00

5. 主食

水饺	5.00	鸡蛋面	2.00
肉丝面	2.00	清汤面	1.50
米饭	1.50	油条	.20/个
馒头	.20/个	煎饼	.30/个

Lesson 14: The Market

In this lesson: *Buying fruit and vegetables by weight. Bargaining. Signs in markets.*

Core Lesson

Dialogue

Foreigner A is in a market. B is a well supplied fruit vendor.

A: Zhè shuǐguǒ xīnxiān ma? (This fruit fresh?)
这水果新鲜吗?

B: Hěn xīnxiān. Yào mǎi duōshao? (Very fresh. Want buy how much?)
很新鲜。要买多少?

A：Xīguā duōshao qián yī jīn?（Watermelon per catty how much?）

西瓜多少钱一斤？

B：Liǎng kuài liù yī jīn. Yào jǐ jīn?（One catty $2.60. Want how many catties?）

两块六一斤。要几斤？

A：Wǔ kuài qián liǎng jīn, hǎo bù hǎo?（Two catties $5.00, okay?）

五块钱两斤，好不好？

B：Xíng, xíng.（OK, OK.）

行，行。

Dialogue Vocabulary

shuǐguǒ (fruit)水果 xīguā (watermelon)西瓜

xīnxiān (fresh)新鲜 jīn (catty)斤

liǎng (tenth of a catty)两 xíng (okay)行

Additional Vocabulary

piányi (inexpensive, cheap)便宜 guì (expensive)贵

gōngjīn (kilogram)公斤 bàn (half)半

***Fruit*:**

píngguǒ (apples)苹果

xiāngjiāo (bananas)香蕉

xīguā (watermelon)西瓜

lí (Chinese pears)梨

táozi (peaches)桃子

chéngzi (orange)橙子

***Vegetables*:**

shūcài (vegetables)蔬菜

húluóbo (carrot)胡萝卜

yángcōng (onion)洋葱

tǔdòu (potato)土豆

báiluóbo (turnip)白萝卜

cōng (green onion)葱

càihuā (cauliflower)菜花

báicài (cabbage)白菜

Useful Phrases

***Bargaining tools*:**

- Piányi yīdiǎn, hǎo bù hǎo?

  (Cheaper a little, okay?)

This sentence is your most basic bargaining tool.

- Tài guì.

  (Too expensive.)

Rather blunt.

● Yǒu yīdiǎn guì.

(Have a little expensive.)

= A bit expensive.

Milder than Tài guì!

● Wǔ kuài qián, hǎo bù hǎo?

(Five yuan, okay not okay?)

= How about five yuan?

● Zhè gè shuǐguǒ huài le.

(This fruit gone bad.)

= This fruit has gone bad.

Sentence Patterns

What is the word order for asking how much something costs by weight?

Pattern: (item) + (amount) + duōshao (qián)?

Examples:

— Jī ròu yī jīn duōshao? (Chicken meat per catty how much?)

— Xiāngjiāo sān jīn duōshao qián? (Bananas three catties how much?)

You will also hear people state the amount after duōshao.

Example: Xīguā duōshao qián yī jīn?

How do you say what something costs by weight?

Pattern: (price) + (amount).

Example:

— Liǎng kuài liù yī jīn. ($2.60 one catty.) = $2.60 per catty.

— Wǔ kuài bā yī jīn. ($5.80 one catty.) = $5.80 per catty.

Notes

***Weight measurements*:**

The main traditional weight measurement used in Chinese markets is the jīn (catty). This is about half a kilogram or a little more than a pound. A liǎng is a tenth of a jīn. These are the measures most often used in the market for buying food. Metric weights, however, are also sometimes used in Chinese markets. The word for kilogram in Chinese is gōngjīn (public catty), so it is sometimes necessary to clarify which kind of jīn one is talking about.

Strategy: Bargaining in markets.

Foreigners sometimes avoid Chinese markets because sentences fly around too fast and you may be worried about getting cheated. However, there are a number of good reasons to become "market literate." First, there is a lot of good food in markets. Second, markets are a great free language class where you can practice a lot of your most basic language tools. Third, bargaining is fun once you have done it a few times and learned the ropes. Finally, having a few vendors at the market who recognize you is a wonderful boost to your sense that you are becoming a part of life in China.

You can often (but not always) bargain at markets or with street vendors, although usually the price won't go down too far (except in tourist areas). Suggestions:

— Try to find out roughly what the price should be before you go to the market so that you will know if the quoted price is outrageous. Note: Produce prices vary by the season and even by the day, so to get good information you need to ask someone who shops in the market often.

— Basic bargaining moves include asking Piányi

yīdiǎn? (Cheaper a little?) or making a counter-offer.

— If you are buying more than one item (and can calculate quickly) a good strategy is to offer the vendor a rounded price that is slightly lower than the original total amount. (This is the strategy A used in the Dialogue above.)

— If the purchase is not vital to you, you can always try walking away. You may get called back with a better offer. And maybe not.

— Finally, become a regular customer and you will probably get a good price right off the bat.

Practice Ideas

Practice with a tutor

***Review*:**

Role play ordering a meal at a restaurant using the menu at the end of the previous lesson. Using the new characters (above) for vegetables and fruits, see if you can read more of the Chinese menu.

***Tones / Pinyin / vocabulary practice*:**

Have your tutor dictate names of other fruits and vegetables to you.

***Role play I*:**

Bargain over fruit in a market. The more stubborn you and your tutor are with each other as you bargain, the more language practice you will get. (Ask your tutor to give you feedback on your strategies as well as on your Chinese.)

***Role play II*:**

Role play buying books from a street seller (bargaining is allowed).

Practice on the street

***RLP*:**

Bargain for fruit or something else at a market.

***RLP*:**

Many nice things like cookies, peanuts, candy, and

sometimes even chocolate can be purchased by weight in some department or general stores. Try buying a bàn jīn (half catty) or so of some such treat.

***Field trip*:**

Have your tutor take you to a market and show you around.

***Sign reading*:**

While in a market, see if you find any of the Survival Characters below.

Extra Credit

Survival Characters

These are characters you may encounter on signs in a market.

斤 jīn(catty)

两 liǎng(tenth of a catty)

公斤 gōngjīn(kilogram)

Colloquial translation of Dialogue

A: Is this fruit fresh?

B: Very fresh. How much do you want to buy?

A: How much is watermelon per catty?

B: ￥2.60 per catty.

A: How about two catties for ￥5.00?

B: Okay, okay.

Lesson 15: The Bus

In this lesson: *Buying tickets* <u>*to*</u> *(some place). Vehicles. Replies to yes/no questions. City maps: bus, train stations, etc.*

Core Lesson

Dialogue

Foreigner A is in a bus station trying to buy a ticket to Nanjing, but isn't sure which is the right ticket window. B is the ticket seller.

A: Zhèr mài bú mài dào Nánjīng de chē piào? (Here sell not sell to Nanjing's vehicle tickets?)
这儿卖不卖到南京的车票?

B：Mài. Nǐ yào jǐdiǎn zhōng de?（Sell. You want what time's?）

卖。你要几点钟的？

A：Sān diǎn bàn de.（Three o'clock half's.）

三点半的。

B：Yào jǐ zhāng?（Want how many?）

要几张？

A：Yī zhāng.（One.）

一张。

A：Dào Nánjīng yào zuò duō jiǔ?（To Nanjing have to sit how long?）

到南京要坐多久？

B：Yī bān lái shuō, sì gè xiǎoshí.（In general, four hours.）

一般来说，四个小时。

Dialogue Vocabulary

mài(to sell)卖　　dào(to)到

chē(vehicle; *here*, bus)车

piào (ticket)票

zhāng (*measure word for tickets*)张

yào (will; need to)要

zuò(to sit;to take a vehicle)坐

yī bān lái shuō (in general, generally speaking)一般来说

Additional Vocabulary

chēzhàn (bus stop, bus station)车站

shàng (up;to get on)上

xià(down;to get off)下

lù(road)路

***Vehicles*:**

chēzi (generic term for vehicle)车子

gōnggòng qìchē(public bus)公共汽车

chūzūchē(taxi; *lit*. rent vehicle)出租车

díshì(taxi)的士

miàn dí(small van taxi)面的

xiǎobā(mini-van; *lit*. small bus)小巴

kǎchē (truck)卡车

huǒchē(train; *lit*. fire vehicle)火车

qìchē (car; *lit*. steam vehicle)汽车

mótuōchē(motorcycle)摩托车

zìxíngchē(bicycle; *lit*. self-propelling vehicle)自行车

***Transportation centers*:**

huǒchē zhàn (train station)火车站

qìchē zhàn (bus station, bus stop)汽车站

fēijī chǎng (airport)飞机场

mǎtou (dock)码头

chángtú chēzhàn (long distance bus station)长途车站

Useful Phrases

- Chēzhàn zài nǎli?

  (Bus stop at where?)

  = Where is the bus stop?

- Shàng chē.

  (Get on bus.)

  = Get on the bus.

- Xià chē.

  (Get off bus.)

  = Get off the bus.

Sentence Patterns

How do I state a destination (like "to Nanjing")?

Pattern: dào + (place).

Examples:

— Dào Nánjīng. (To Nanjing.)

— Dào huǒchē zhàn, zuò jǐ lù chē? (To train station, take which number bus?)

— Dào fēijīchǎng, zuò shénme chē? (To airport, take what vehicle?)

How do I say "the bus (or whatever) to ___"?

Pattern: dào + (destination) + (possessive).

Examples:

— Dào Běijīng de huǒchē zài nǎli? (To Beijing's train at where?) = Where is the train to Beijing?

— Zhè gè xiǎo bā shì bú shì dào shūdiàn de? (This mini-van is not is to bookstore's?) = Is this the mini-van to the bookstore?

Notes

***Buying bus tickets*:**

The price of a trip often varies according to distance, and the conductor may ask you where you are going, so knowing a place name helps. (However, more and more Chinese cities now have buses where you simply drop a fixed amount into the box as you get on the bus.)

***Mini-vans*:**

These generally have the same numbers and follow the same routes as regular buses, but unlike regular buses you can usually wave these down at almost any point along their route (though this is changing in larger cities). Mini-vans generally cost more than buses.

***Tip*: *Mistakes and learning grammar*.**

One of the best ways to learn grammar is through experimentation. The process by which people most naturally learn grammar is called successive approximation; in other words, at first people use simple but flawed sentences and gradually refine them by trial and error until they become more accurate and complex.

It is not only okay to make lots of mistakes in conversation, but virtually necessary if you are to do the kind of grammar experimentation that is necessary for learning, so one of the best ways to learn is by plunging in and speaking at every opportunity. It is less important that you get every sentence right than that you learn from your mistakes.

Practice Activities

Practice with a tutor

***Review*:**

Role play buying fruit and vegetables with your tutor.

***Tones / Pinyin / vocabulary*:**

Have your tutor dictate a number of important Chinese city names to you.

Usage:

Practice making sentences with yào.

Role play:

Role play buying tickets to cities in China.

Map reading:

Locate local transportation centers using the "Transportation Center" characters above.

Practice on the street

RLP:

Practice asking people where local buses go.

Field trip:

Have a Chinese friend take you somewhere on a bus. Make sure you do the talking.

Field trip:

Using a city map, find and visit the transportation centers in your city.

Extra Credit

Survival Characters

It is useful to be able to locate transportation centers on a map, especially if you are planning to travel. (See "Transportation centers" above.)

Colloquial translation of Dialogue

A: Do you sell bus tickets to Nanjing here?

B: Yes. Which bus do you want?

A: The 3:30 one.

B: How many tickets?

A: One. How long does it take to Nanjing?

B: In general, four hours.

Lesson 16: The Taxi

In this lesson: *Giving directions to taxis. "Is it permitted to ____?" Making suggestions. Signs: taxi stands.*

Core Lesson

Dialogue

Foreigner A is headed to the museum and waves down a taxi; B is the taxi driver.

B: Dào nǎli? (To where?)

到哪里?

A: Dào bówùguǎn. Qǐng nǐ dǎ biǎo. (To museum. Please start meter.)

到博物馆。请你打表。

……………………

A：Qǐng nǐ tíng chē.（Please stop the taxi.）

请你停车。

B：Zhèr bù kěyǐ tíng chē.（Here not permitted stop taxi.）

这儿不可以停车。

B：Wǒ zài qiánmian tíng chē ba.（I at ahead stop car, how's that?）

我在前面停车吧。

A：Hǎo ba.（Okay.）

好吧。

Dialogue Vocabulary

bówùguǎn（museum）博物馆

dǎ（to hit; to start a meter）打

biǎo（meter）表

tíng（to stop）停

kěyǐ（may; permitted to）可以

ba（*suggestion particle*）吧

Additional Vocabulary

guǎi wān(to turn a corner)拐弯

zǒu (to walk, to go, to leave)走

chōu yān(to smoke)抽烟

lù(road)路

zǒu lù(to walk)走路

Useful Phrases

- Yǒu méiyǒu biǎo?

  (Have not have meter?)

  = Do you have a meter?

This is a good question for not only checking to see if a vehicle has a meter — and is thus a legal taxi — but also for suggesting that the meter be used.)

- Kàn biǎo ba.

  (Look meter, okay.)

  = Let's go according to the meter (price), okay?

Useful if a taxi driver starts trying to negotiate a price instead of using the meter.

- Dào fēijīchǎng duōshao qián?

  (To airport, how much?)

For more distant destinations such as airports, the price sometimes needs to be negotiated.

- Dào le!

  (Arrived!)

  = We're there!

Useful for telling a taxi driver he/she can stop.

Sentence Patterns

How do I say that doing something is (not) permitted (somewhere)?

Pattern: (place) + (bù) kěyǐ + (action).

Examples:

— Zhèr kěyǐ tíng chē. (Here permitted to stop vehicle.) = It's permitted to stop the vehicle here.

— Zài bówùguǎn bù kěyǐ chōu yān. (In museum not permitted to smoke.) = You aren't allowed to smoke in the museum.

— Zài qiánmian kěyǐ guǎi wān ma? (Ahead

permitted to turn?) = Can we turn up ahead?

Notice in Chinese word order that the place comes first.

How do I make a suggestion?

Another way to make a suggestion is with the particle bɑ.

Pattern: (sentence) + bɑ.

Examples:

— Wǒmen chī fàn bɑ. (We eat, okay.) = Let's eat.

— Wǒmen zǒu bɑ. (We go, okay.) = Let's leave.

— Wǒmen zǒu lù bɑ. (We walk, okay.) = Let's walk.

— Wǒmen míngtiān qù bówùguǎn bɑ. (We tomorrow go museum, okay.) = Let's go to the museum tomorrow.

Notes

Chē:

In Chinese the words chē and chēzi are used much more often than the word "vehicle" is in English. In fact, whereas in English one usually says "car", "bus" or whatever, in Chinese the more general word chēzi is often used, with context clarifying what kind of vehicle is in question.

Strategy: Negotiating taxis.

Your ability to get around Chinese cities expands dramatically once you become comfortable using Chinese taxis, so this is a skill worth developing as soon as possible. In general you don't need to worry much about overcharging by taxi drivers in China, but there are always a few exceptions and it would be too bad if concern about being overcharged were to cause you to avoid taxis. A few suggestions for minimizing problems:

— Regular taxis (those with meters) are less likely to overcharge than those which lack meters.

— It is better to get a taxi at a regular taxi stand or to hail one on the street than it is to go with a taxi driver who hustles business at places like train and bus stations. (These locations generally have a regular taxi stand, though you may need to look for it. If you can't find one, you might want to walk a little distance from the station before hailing a taxi.)

— For more distant destinations such as airports,

taxis often don't charge according to the meter. For these destinations it is especially important to find out in advance what would be a fair price according to local custom.

Practice Ideas

Practice with a tutor

***Review*:**

Practice buying a bus ticket.

***Usage*:**

Practice making sentences with kěyǐ.

***Role play*:**

Role play taking a taxi to various locations. Tell the taxi driver where you want to go, clarify the price, and tell him/her to stop. (You might also ask your tutor for suggestions as to how to deal with drivers who overcharge.)

Practice on the street

***RLP*:**

Take a solo taxi ride to some place in the city. (Before setting out, check with a Chinese friend to see approximately how much it should cost to take a taxi to these destinations.)

***Field trip*:**

Have a Chinese friend show you some of the places in your neighborhood where it is relatively easy to get a taxi.

Extra Credit

Survival Characters

To locate a taxi stand on the street, learn the following characters:

出租车 chūzūchē (taxi)　　　　的士 díshì (taxi)

Colloquial translation of Dialogue

B: Where are you going?

A: To the museum. Please use the meter.

....

A: Please stop the cab.

B: I can't stop here. I'll stop up ahead, okay?

A: Okay.

Lesson 17: Post Office (II)

In this lesson: *Getting packages. "Did you ____?" Verbs for getting, bringing. ID's and certificates.*

Core Lesson

Dialogue

Foreigner A arrives at the post office with package notice clutched firmly in hand. B is a postal worker.

A: Wǒ lái ná bāoguǒ. (I come get package.)

我来拿包裹。

B: Bāoguǒ dān ne? (Package notice?)

包裹单呢?

A: Zài zhèr. (Here.)

在这儿。

B：Yǒu méiyǒu dài gōngzuòzhèng?（Did or didn't bring work card?）

有没有带工作证?

A：Duìbuqǐ，wǒ méiyǒu dài.（Sorry，I didn't bring.）

对不起，我没有带。

B：Yǒu méiyǒu hùzhào?（Have not have passport?）

有没有护照?

A：Yǒu. Děng yīxià.（Have. Wait a minute.）

有。等一下。

Dialogue Vocabulary

ná（to get，to pick up，to carry）拿

bāoguǒ（package）包裹

bāoguǒ dān（package notice）包裹单

dài（to take，to bring）带

gōngzuòzhèng（work card）工作证

hùzhào（passport）护照

Additional Vocabulary

pái duì（to stand in line）排队

wàngjì（to forget）忘记

dānwèi（work unit）单位

dōngxi(thing)东西

Useful Phrases

- Wǒ wàngjì le.
  (I forgot.)

- Zài nǎli pái duì?
  (At where stand in line?)
  = Where should I line up?

In front of the various windows in a post office, you may see little crowds rather than lines, but this is still how you ask which one you should get into.

Sentence Patterns

How do I say "*Did you* (*do something*) *or not*?"

Pattern: (subject) + yǒu méiyǒu + (verb) + (object).

Examples:

— Nǐ yǒu méiyǒu dài gōngzuòzhèng? (You have not have bring work card?) = Did you bring your work card or not?

— Nǐ yǒu méiyǒu dài qián? (You have not have

bring money?) = Did you bring any money?

— Nǐ zuótiān yǒu méiyǒu qù yóujú? (You yesterday have not have gone post office?) = Did you go to the post office yesterday?

How do I say "I didn't (do something)"?

Pattern: méiyǒu + (predicate).

Examples:

— Wǒ méiyǒu dài qián. (I have not brought money.) = I didn't bring any money.

— Wǒ méiyǒu qù. (I not have gone.) = I didn't go.

"*I did go" would be* Wǒ qù le.

Notes

Ne:

Note how ne is used in the Dialogue above, where little explanation is needed because context makes things clear.

Dài *and* ná:

While the usage of these two words overlaps, there is also some difference:

Dài usually means to carry on one's person, "to

bring/take with one."

Examples:

— Nǐ dài le duōshao qián?

(You brought how much money?)

= How much money did you bring?

— Wǒ wàngjì dài qián.

(I forgot to bring/take money.)

= I forgot to bring money (with me).

Ná usually means to get/take something, and also refers to the physical act of carrying something.

Examples:

— Tā wàngjì ná qián.

(He forgot to get money.)

= He forgot to get money (from somewhere).

— Wǒ yào qù ná bāoguǒ.

(I am going to go get package.)

= I am going to get a package (from somewhere).

— Nà gè dōngxi bù hǎo ná.

(That thing not good carry.)

= That thing is hard to carry.

Practice Ideas

Practice with a tutor

***Review*:**

Role play a trip in a taxi. Make it more exciting by having the driver try to extort extra money from the passenger.

***Usage*:**

Practice making sentences using ná and dài.

***Role play*:**

Role play picking up a package at the post office.

***ID reading*:**

With your tutor look at some Chinese documents such as residence permits, visas, ID cards, and so forth. Locate vital things like expiration dates.

Practice on the street

RLP:

Go to the post office yourself and figure out where you would pick up a package. If you actually have one to pick up, so much the better.

Extra Credit

Survival Characters

The Chinese words for many kinds of documentation and certificates end with zhèng (certificate):

工作证 gōngzuòzhèng (work card)
居留证 jūliúzhèng (residence permit)
签证 qiānzhèng (visa)
专家证 zhuānjiāzhèng (foreign expert card)

Colloquial translation of Dialogue

A: I've come to get a package.

B: The package notice?

A: Here.

B: Did you bring your work card?

A: Sorry, I didn't bring it.

B: Do you have a passport?

A: Yes. Wait a minute.

Lesson 18: Not Feeling Well

In this lesson: *Health problems. Parts of the body. Medicines. City maps: hospitals.*

Core Lesson

Dialogue

At the guesthouse where she is staying, foreigner A is not feeling well and is explaining to staff person B that she wants to see a doctor.

A: Wǒ xiǎng kàn yīshēng. (I want to see a doctor.)
我想看医生。

B: Nǐ nǎli bù shūfu? (You where uncomfortable?)

你哪里不舒服？

A：Wǒ de wèi hěn tòng.（My stomach very painful.）

我的胃很痛。

B：Nǐ yǒu méiyǒu chī yào?（You have not have eaten medicine?）

你有没有吃药？

A：Wǒ méiyǒu yào.（I don't have medicine.）

我没有药。

B：Wǒ dài nǐ qù yīyuàn.（I take you go to hospital.）

我带你去医院。

Dialogue Vocabulary

yīshēng(doctor)医生　　shūfu(comfortable)舒服

wèi(stomach)胃　　tòng(to hurt, to be painful)痛

yào(medicine)药　　yīyuàn(hospital)医院

Additional Vocabulary

zěnmele(what's wrong)怎么了

bìng(illness; to be sick)病

gǎnmào (a cold; to have a cold)感冒

lā dùzi(diarrhea; to have diarrhea)拉肚子

guà hào(to register at hospital)挂号

dìfang(place)地方

suān(sore)酸

yǎng(itch;itchy)痒

***Parts of the body*:**

tóu(head)头

ěrduo(ears)耳朵

bízi(nose)鼻子

shǒu(hand,arm)手

bèi(back)背

dùzi(abdomen)肚子

tuǐ(leg)腿

yáchǐ(tooth)牙齿

yǎnjīng(eyes)眼睛

zuǐbā(mouth)嘴巴

hóulóng(throat)喉咙

bózi(neck)脖子

xiōngkǒu(chest)胸口

jiǎo(foot)脚

pífū(skin)皮肤

Useful Phrases

- Nǐ zěnmela?

  (You how?)

  = What's wrong with you?

Said sympathetically, this is the appropriate inquiry to a person who looks sick or upset. In a sharper tone of voice, it can also be an accusing question about someone's mental competence.

- Wǒ xiǎng kàn bìng.

  (I want to see illness.)

  = I want to see a doctor.

- Wǒ bìng le.

  (I have become sick.)

- Wǒ gǎnmào.

  (I have a cold.)

- Wǒ lā dùzi.

  (I pull abdomen.)

  = I have diarrhea.

- Zài nǎli guà hào?

  (At where register?)

  = Where do I register?

In a Chinese hospital or clinic, you need to register before seeing a doctor.

Sentence Patterns

What is the sentence pattern for saying some part of my body hurts?

Pattern: Wǒ de + (part of body) + (problem).

Examples:

— Wǒ de wèi tòng. (My stomach hurts.)

— Wǒ de jiǎo suān. (My foot sore.) = My foot is sore.

— Wǒ de wèi bù shūfu. (My stomach uncomfortable.) = My stomach doesn't feel good.

— Wǒ de yǎnjing yǒu wèntí. (My eye has problem.) = There's something wrong with my eye.

— Wǒ de pífū hěn yǎng. (My skin very itchy.)

For the pattern above, the following words can all be used in the "problem" slot:

— bù shūfu (not comfortable)

— suān (sore)

— yǎng (itchy)

— yǒu wèntí (have a problem)

Notes

Shūfu:

This is also the general term for "comfortable."

Example:

Zhè gè dìfang hěn shūfu.

(This place very comfortable.)

= This place is very comfortable.

Chī yào:

Notice that in Chinese you "eat" medicine.

Practice Ideas

Practice with a tutor

Review:

Role play picking up a package at the post office.

Tones / Pinyin / vocabulary:

Point to parts of your body and have your tutor dictate the proper words in Chinese. Then as your tutor points to body parts, call out the proper word in

Chinese. Have your tutor start with words you know, adding new ones as you get quicker on the old ones.

***Usage*:**

Experiment with sentences describing health problems.

***Role play*:**

First, role play getting someone to take you to a clinic or hospital. Then role play seeing a doctor and explaining your health problem(s).

***Map reading*:**

Locate hospitals on your city map.

Practice on the street

***Field trip*:**

Have a Chinese friend show you a nearby hospital (clinic, etc.) and even walk you through the registration process.

Extra Credit

Survival Characters

For obvious reasons, it is good to be able to locate and identify hospitals, both on maps and in your vicinity.

医院 yīyuàn (hospital)　　　医务室 yīwùshì (clinic)

Extra Credit Vocabulary

***Health problems*:**

Problems using the same sentence pattern are grouped together. (Chinese characters are omitted under the assumption that you are more likely to need to say these things than read them.)

lā dùzi (to have diarrhea)

Ex: Wǒ lā dùzi. (I have diarrhea.)

gǎnmào (to have a cold)

Ex: Wǒ gǎnmào. (I have a cold.)

fāshāo(to have a fever)

Ex: Wǒ fāshāo. (I have a fever.)

biànmì(to be constipated)

Ex: Wǒ biànmì. (I'm constipated.)

tóu tòng(to have a headache)

Ex: Wǒ tóu tòng. (My head hurts.) = I have a headache.

késou(to cough)

Ex: Wǒ késou. (I cough.) = I have a cough.

dàbiàn(feces; to defecate)

Ex: Wǒ dàbiàn yǒu wèntí. (My defecation has problems.) = I have trouble with my bowel movements.

xiǎobiàn(urine; to urinate)

Ex: Wǒ xiǎobiàn yǒu wèntí. (My urination has problems.) = I have trouble urinating.

zhǒng(to swell)

Ex: Wǒ de tuǐ zhǒng le. (My leg has swollen.)

duàn(to break)

Ex: Wǒ de tuǐ duàn le. (My leg has broken.)

tán(mucus)

Ex: Tán hěn duō. (Mucus very much.) = There's a lot of mucus.

***Chinese Names of Common Medicines*:**

The list below includes both some general medicine names and some names of familiar Western brands.[1]

Pain relievers(zhǐ tòng yào)止痛药

Tylenol(tài nuò lín)泰诺林

Panadol(bì lǐ tōng)必理通

Tramal(qū mǎ duō)曲马多

Bufferin(bǎi fú níng)百服宁

aspirin(ā sī pǐ lín)阿司匹林

Anti-inflammatory drugs(xiāo yán yào)消炎药

Fenbid(fēn bì dé)芬必得

Ibuprofen(bù luó fēn)布罗芬

Cold medicines(gǎnmào yào)感冒药

Tylenol Cold(tài nuò)泰诺

---

1 Thanks to Joy Hilbun for compiling this list.

Antihistimines(kàng zǔ'àn)抗组胺

Antibiotics(kàng shēng sù)抗生素

erythromycin(hóng méi sù)红霉素

ampicillin(ān bì xiān)安必仙

amoxycillin(ā mò líng)阿莫灵

Vitamins(wéi shēng sù piàn)维生素片

Gold Theragran(Squibb)(jīn shī ěr kāng)金施尔康

Diarrhea Medicine(zhǐ xiè yào)止泻药

Imodium(yì méng tíng)易蒙停

Anti-nausea medicine(kàng ě xīn yào)抗恶心药

Antacids(kàng suān jì)抗酸剂

Miscellaneous

cortisone(kě di sōng)可的松 or (kǎo di sōng)考的松

anti-fungal(kàng zhēn jūn)抗真菌

mercurochrome(hóng yào shuǐ)红药水

analgesic cream(like Ben Gay)(jī ròu zhǐ tòng gāo)肌肉止痛膏

Colloquial translation of Dialogue

A: I want to see a doctor.

B: Where do you feel bad?

A: My stomach hurts a lot.

B: Have you taken any medicine?

A: I don't have any medicine.

B: I'll take you to the hospital.

Lesson 19: Changing Money

In this lesson: "*Where can I ____?*" *Possibilities. Comparisons. Signs: services in banks.*

Core Lesson

Dialogue

Foreigner A needs to change money and accosts Chinese person B on the street to find out what the best place to change money is.

A: Qǐng wèn, nǎli kěyǐ huàn qián? (May I ask, where possible to change money?)
请问,哪里可以换钱?

B: Jiǔdiàn, yínháng, dōu kěyǐ. (Hotel, bank, both

possible.）

酒店、银行，都可以。

A：Nǎ gè bǐjiào hǎo?（Which one relatively better?）

哪个比较好？

B：Yínháng bǐ jiǔdiàn jìn.（Bank compared to hotel close.）

银行比酒店近。

B：Dànshì, jiǔdiàn kěnéng bǐjiào fāngbiàn.（But hotel possibly relatively convenient.）

但是酒店可能比较方便。

B：Tāmen kěndìng néng jiǎng Yīngyǔ.（They definitely able to speak English.）

他们肯定能讲英语。

B：Tāmen de duìhuànlǜ yě kěnéng gāo yīdiǎn.（Their exchange rate also possibly high a little.）

他们的兑换率也可能高一点。

B：…dànshì zhè gè wǒ bú tài qīngchu.（... but this I not too sure.）

……但是这个我不太清楚。

Dialogue Vocabulary

huàn (to exchange; to change)换

jiǔdiàn(hotel)酒店

yínháng(bank)银行

dōu(both, all)都

bǐjiào (comparatively, relatively)比较

bǐ(compared to)比

dànshì(but)但是

kěnéng(possible; possibly)可能

fāngbiàn(convenient)方便

kěndìng(definitely)肯定

néng(able to)能

jiǎng(to speak)讲

duìhuànlǜ(exchange rate)兑换率

gāo(high, tall)高

tài(too)太

qīngchu(clear, sure about)清楚

Additional Vocabulary

xiě(to write)写

guì(expensive)贵

shǔ(to count)数

Useful Phrases

- Wǒ bú tài qīngchu.

(I'm not too clear.)

= I'm not too sure.

- Duìhuànlǜ duōshao?

  (Exchange rate how much?)

  = What is the exchange rate?

- Qǐng nǐ xiě yīxià.

  (Please you write a bit.)

  = Please write it down.

If you don't trust your ears in getting an exchange rate, this request is very useful.

- Qǐng nǐ shǔ yī shǔ.

  (Please you count one count.)

  = Please count it.

Bank clerks may ask you to do this when handing you your money.

Sentence Patterns

How do I ask "Where can I ____?"

Pattern: Nǎli + kěyǐ + (verb) + (object)?

Examples:

— Nǎli kěyǐ huàn qián? (Where can change money?) = Where can (I) change money?

— Nǎli kěyǐ chī fàn? (Where can eat rice?) = Where can (we) get something to eat?

— Nǎli kěyǐ kàn bìng? (Where can see illness?) = Where can (I) see a doctor?

How do I compare two things?

Pattern: A + bǐ + B + (adjective).

Examples:

— Yínháng bǐ jiǔdiàn jìn. (Bank than hotel close.) = The bank is closer than the hotel.

— Tā bǐ wǒ gāo. (He/she than me tall.) = He/she is taller than me.

— Nǐ bǐ wǒ hǎo. (You than I better.) = You are better than I am.

— Tā bǐ wǒ yǒu qián. (He/she than I has money.) = He/she has more money than I do.

How else can I compare two things?

Another way to compare is by using yīdiǎn (a little).

Pattern: (adjective) + yīdiǎn.

Examples:

— Tāmen de duìhuànlǜ gāo yīdiǎn. (Their exchange rate high a little.) = Their exchange rate is a little higher.

— Qǐng nǐ jiǎng màn yīdiǎn. (Please you speak slow a little.) = Please speak a little slower.

— Zhè gè xīguā guì yīdiǎn. (This watermelon expensive a little.) = This watermelon is a little more expensive.

Notes

jiǎng:

This word is interchangeable with shuō.

tài:

This means "too" as in "too much."

Exchanging money:

Not all banks change foreign currency. Usually your best bet is Zhōngguó Yínháng (the Bank of China), but sometimes you can change money in other banks or in large hotels. (You may also encounter people on the street who want to exchange money, but this is both risky and illegal.)

Practice Ideas

Practice with a tutor

***Review*:**

Practice getting an illness treated by a doctor.

***Tone/Pinyin practice*:**

Have your tutor dictate the names of different currencies while you write them down in *Pinyin*.

***Usage*:**

Practice making comparisons using bǐjiào, A bǐ B ____, and (adjective) + yīdiǎn.

***Role play*:**

Role play changing money at a bank.

***Map reading*:**

Using the Survival Characters, locate banks on your

city map.

Practice on the street

***RLP*:**

Try changing money at a bank.

***Field trip*:**

Have a Chinese friend show you around a bank and explain the services provided.

***Sign reading*:**

In a bank, look for the windows where exchange and savings services are offered.

Extra Credit

Survival Characters

The following characters may help you locate banking services:

银行 yínháng(bank)

中国银行 Zhōngguó Yínháng(Bank of China)

兑换 duìhuàn(money exchange)

存款 cúnkuǎn(savings)

Extra Credit Vocabulary

***Commonly encountered currencies*:**

Rénmínbì(Chinese currency)人民币

Měiyuán(US currency)美元

Gǎngbì(Hong Kong currency)港币

Rìyuán(Japanese currency)日元

Colloquial translation of Dialogue

A: Excuse me, where can I change money?

B: Either at a hotel or a bank.

A: Which is better?

B: The bank is closer than the hotel. But the hotel may be more convenient. They can surely speak English. Their exchange rate may also be a little higher, but I'm not too sure.

Lesson 20: A Long Distance Phone Call

In this lesson: *Making a long distance phone call. "Is ____ there?" Dealing with phone call problems. Computer services. "How do I ____?" Signs: telecommunications center services.*

Core Lesson

Dialogue

Foreigner A wants to make a long distance phone call in a small hotel in China. B works at the front desk. C is the operator at the hotel A calls, and D is Mr. Tang.

A：Qǐng wèn，chángtú diànhuà zěnme dǎ?（May I ask, long distance phone call, how to make?）

请问，长途电话怎么打？

B：Diànhuà hàomǎ duōshao?（Phone number, how much?）

电话号码多少？

B：Wǒ bāng nǐ dǎ.（I help you call.）

我帮你打。

A：Bú yòng. Wǒ zìjǐ dǎ.（Not necessary. I myself call.）

不用。我自己打。

....

A：（*On phone*）Jīnshān Jiǔdiàn ma?（Golden Mountain Hotel?）

金山酒店吗？

C：Qǐng shuō dà shēng yīdiǎn，wǒ tīng bú jiàn.（Please speak louder a little, I listen not hear.）

请说大声一点，我听不见。

A：（*Louder*）Jīnshān Jiǔdiàn ma?（Golden Mountain Hotel?）

金山酒店吗？

C：Shì. Nǐ zhǎo shéi?（Is. You look for who?）

是。你找谁？

A：Qǐng zhuǎn sān líng liù fáng.（Please forward 306

room.)

请转三零六房。

....

D：Wèi!（Hello!）

喂!

A：Táng xiānsheng zài bú zài?（Tang Mr. there not there?）

唐先生在不在?

D：Wǒ shì.（I am.）

我是。

Dialogue Vocabulary

chángtú(long distance)长途

diànhuà (phone, phone call)电话

zěnme(how)怎么

dǎ(to hit)打

dǎ diànhuà(make a phone call)打电话

hàomǎ(number)号码

yòng(to use)用

bú yòng(it's not necessary)不用

zìjǐ(self;myself)自己

dà shēng(loud)大声

zhǎo(to look for)找

shéi(who)谁

zhuǎn(to forward)转

fáng(room)房

wèi(hello)喂

xiānsheng(mister)先生

Additional Vocabulary

cuò(wrong)错

zài(again)再

qīngchu(clear)清楚

jiǎng(to speak, to say)讲

diànhuà hàomǎ (phone number)电话号码

fēnjī hàomǎ (extension number)分机号码

wàiguórén(foreigner)外国人

fángjiān(a room)房间

***Computer Vocabulary*:**

diànnǎo(computer)电脑

diànzǐ yóujiàn(e-mail)电子邮件

wǎngluò(the internet)网络

shàngwǎng(to go on-line)上网

ruǎnjiàn(software)软件

zhuāng ruǎnjiàn(to install software)装软件

wǎngbā(internet cafe)网吧

Useful Phrases

- Nǐ dǎ cuò le.

  (You called wrong.)

= You called the wrong number.

● Nǐ huì bú huì shuō Yīngyǔ?

(You can/cannot speak English?)

= Can you speak English?

This sentence is useful if a Chinese speaker answers the phone and you need to hint that you would like to speak to someone who knows English.

Also:

Nǐ huì bú huì jiǎng Yīngyǔ?

● Qǐng nǐ zài shuō yí biàn.

(Please you again say once.)

= Please say that once again.

● Wǒ shì wàiguórén. Wǒ tīng bù dǒng.

(I am foreigner. I don't understand.)

This sentence is useful when you answer the phone and find yourself bombarded with more Chinese than you are ready to handle yet.

● Qǐng nǐ shuō dà shēng yīdiǎn.

(Please you speak loud a little.)

= Please speak a little louder.

Also:

— Qǐng nǐ shuō màn yīdiǎn. (Please you speak slow a little.) = Please speak a little slower.

— Qǐng nǐ shuō qīngchu yīdiǎn. (Please you speak clear a little.) = Please speak a little more clearly.

In any of the sentences above, shuō *can be replaced with* jiǎng.

Survival Characters

How do I ask how to do something?

Pattern: (subject) + zěnme + (verb)?

Examples:

— Chángtú diànhuà zěnme dǎ? (Long distance phone call how to make?) = How do you make a long distance phone call?

— Zhè zhǒng dōngxi zěnme mǎi? (This kind of thing how to buy?) = How do you buy something like this?

— Shànghǎi zěnme qù? (Shanghai how to go?) = How do you get to Shanghai?

How do I say I want to do something myself?

Pattern: (pronoun) + zìjǐ + (verb).

The sentence pattern is often used when emphasizing that one can/will do something for oneself, and doesn't need assistance.

Examples:

— Wǒ zìjǐ dǎ. (I'll myself make.) = I'll make (the call) myself.

— Wǒ zìjǐ mǎi. (I'll myself buy.) = I'll buy it myself (instead of you buying it for me).

— Nǐ zìjǐ qù ba. (You yourself go.) = Why don't you go yourself (instead of me going for you)?

— Wǒ zìjǐ lái. (I myself come.) = I'll do it myself.

This last sentence should be memorized as a whole.

How do I ask an operator for an extension?

Pattern: Qǐng zhuǎn + (#).

Examples:

— Qǐng zhuǎn èr bā liù. (Please forward to #286.) = (Extension) 286 please.

How do I ask an operator for a room number?

Pattern: Qǐng zhuǎn + (#) + fáng.

Examples:

— Qǐng zhuǎn sān líng liù fáng. (Please forward #306 room.) = Room 306 please.

— Qǐng zhuǎn sì bā jiǔ fáng. (Please forward to #489 room.) = Room #489 please.

Notice that fáng *is added after the room number*.

Notes

Wèi!

This word is normally only used on the telephone, though you will occasionally hear people use it in other settings to attract someone's attention.

Tīng bú jiàn:

This means "I can't hear," as opposed to tīng bù dǒng (I can't understand).

Phone numbers:

Phone numbers are most easily stated by just listing the numbers; there is no need to combine them into groups.

***Phones*:**

Some people in China have extensions rather than direct lines, so when calling friends it really helps to be able to say to the operator: Qǐng zhuǎn ____.

Strategy: *Using the phone in Chinese*.

Using a phone in a foreign language tends to be intimidating because the sound often isn't clear and you can't see the expression and gestures of whoever you are talking to. However, when the phone rings you have one great advantage — predictability. The first question the caller will ask 90% of the time is "Is so-and-so there?" so successfully answering the phone is largely a matter of having strategies to get the caller to slow down and let you clearly hear the name of the person they want to talk to. Likewise, making a phone call mainly involves getting to the right extension and then finding out if the person you want to talk to is there or not. Most of the time the few basic sentences in this lesson will get you where you want to go.

Practice Ideas

Practice with a tutor

***Review*:**

Practice changing money at a bank.

***Tones / Pinyin / vocabulary*:**

Give your tutor a list of cities where you know people you might call, and have her/him dictate the Chinese names of these cities. (Having a map handy would help, especially if you want the name of a place that is not a major capital.)

***Usage*:**

Practice making sentences with zìjǐ.

***Role play*:**

Practice making and answering phone calls. Practice until the basic phrases you will need come quickly and easily. When you feel ready, have your tutor go to a phone nearby and actually call you a few times until you get used to hearing Chinese over the telephone.

***Map reading*:**

Using the Survival Characters, locate the local telecommunications center on a city map.

Practice on the street

***RLP*:**

Make a phone call to a Chinese friend.

***RLP*:**

Make a long-distance call to a friend elsewhere in China.

***Field trip*:**

Locate public phones in your neighborhood where you can make either in-country or international long distance phone calls.

***Field trip*:**

Have a Chinese friend tour you through a

telecommunications center with computer and/or long-distance phone facilities. Practice reading the signs.

Extra Credit

Survival Characters

In a Chinese telecommunications center or even on the street, being able to read the following characters will help you locate phone services.

电话　　diànhuà(telephone)
长途　　chángtú(long distance)
国际　　guójì(international)
直拨　　zhí bō(direct dial)
电信局　diàn xìn jú(telecom center)
电脑　　diànnǎo(computer)

Colloquial translation of Dialogue

A: Excuse me, how do I make a long distance phone call?

B: What is the phone number? I'll place the call for

you.

A: That's not necessary. I'll place it myself.

…………

A: (*On phone*) Is this the Golden Mountain Hotel?

C: Please speak a little louder, I can't hear you.

A: (*Louder*) Is this the Golden Mountain Hotel?

C: Yes. Who do you wish to speak to?

A: Please forward me to Room 306.

…………

D: Hello!

A: Is Mr. Tang there?

D: Speaking.

Lesson 21: Politely Refusing Requests

In this lesson: *Requests foreigners often hear in China. Making excuses. Apologizing.*

Core Lesson

Dialogue

Foreigner A, an English teacher, is shopping in a store. Chinese person B comes up and starts conversation.

B: Nǐ shì Měiguórén mɑ? (You are American?)
你是美国人吗?

A: Shì de. (Am.)

是的。

B：Wǒ zài xué Yīngyǔ,…（I am learning English...）

我在学英语……

B：…dànshì wǒ méiyǒu jīhuì liànxí.（... but I don't have opportunity to practice.）

但是我没有机会练习。

B：Nǐ yuànyì jiāo wǒ Yīngyǔ ma?（You willing to teach me English?）

你愿意教我英语吗？

A：Duìbuqǐ…（Sorry...）

对不起……

A：Wǒ zài xuéxiào yǐjīng yǒu hěn duō xuéshēng.（I at school already have many students.）

我在学校已经有很多学生。

B：Nàme, wǒ xīngqītiān qù zhǎo nǐ hǎo ma?（Then, I Sundays go look for you, okay?）

那么，我星期天去找你好吗？

A：Hěn bàoqiàn. Wǒ shízài tài máng.（Very apologetic. I really too busy.）

很抱歉。我实在太忙。

Dialogue Vocabulary

jīhuì(opportunity)机会
liànxí(to practice)练习
yuànyì(to be willing)愿意
yǐjīng(already)已经
nàme (well, in that case...)那么
xīngqītiān(Sunday)星期天
zhǎo(to look for; to visit)找
bàoqiàn(apologetic)抱歉
shízài(really, truly)实在
máng(busy)忙

Additional Vocabulary

jiāohuàn(to exchange)交换
zuò(to be, to become)做
péngyou(friend)朋友
shíjiān(time)时间
kòng(free time)空

Useful Phrases

***Requests*:**

Two requests foreigners often encounter in China are:

- Wǒ xiǎng liànxí Yīngyǔ.
  (I want to practice English.)

- Wǒmen zuò péngyou ba.

  (We be friends, okay?)

  = Let's become friends.

***Responses*:**

If you want to refuse or negotiate the requests above, the following phrases may be helpful:

- Wǒ hěn máng.

  (I very busy.)

- Wǒ de gōngzuò hěn máng.

  (My work very busy.)

  = I have a lot of work to do.

- Wǒ méiyǒu shíjiān.

  (I don't have time.)

- Wǒ méiyǒu kòng.

  (I don't have free time.)

- Wǒmen jiāohuàn, hǎo ma?

(We exchange, okay?)

This sentence is useful if you want to do an exchange, for example, English lessons for Chinese.

Notes

Shì de:

In this answer to a yes/no question, the de is optional.

Strategy: Refusing requests.

One problem that foreigners who want to learn Chinese often have in China is the many eager students who would love to practice English with a foreigner. There is thus a fairly good chance that you will get more offers to practice English than you care to accept, sometimes from randomly encountered total strangers. When you want to refuse, the most common strategy is generally to plead that you are too busy — this excuse is not offensive and is fairly understandable. Suitors may not give up easily, but if you politely persist you can usually prevail.

Tip: Focusing your efforts.

As you move into your work, you will probably have less time for Chinese study and your progress in Chinese may well slow down. This is especially a problem if you maintain a full program of Chinese study, working simultaneously on speaking, listening, reading, and writing, because the more spread out your efforts are, the less progress you will feel in any particular skill area, and the greater the chance that you will become discouraged and quit.

One solution is to devote enough time to Chinese study that you still make satisfactory progress in all areas. However, an alternative which is often more realistic is to narrow the range of your efforts, for example, by just working on speaking and listening for a period of time, or by focussing heavily on characters for a while. Having a sense of progress is vitally important in maintaining the will to keep studying, and the narrower the range of your efforts is, the more progress you will see in that one area.

Practice Ideas

Practice with a tutor

***Review*:**

With your tutor, role play making a long distance phone call.

***Usage*:**

Practice making sentences with yuànyì and shízài.

***Role play*:**

Have your tutor try to persuade you to give free English lessons while you fend off the attempts. Then switch roles, with you begging shamelessly for Chinese practice.

Practice on the street

***RLP*:**

Ask some Chinese person (a guesthouse staff member, store clerk, etc.) to practice a little Chinese with you.

Colloquial translation of Dialogue

B : Are you an American?

A : Yes.

B : I'm studying English, but I don't have a chance to practice. Are you willing to teach me English?

A : Sorry. I already have many students at school.

B : In that case, how about if I visit you on Sundays?

A : I'm sorry. I'm really too busy.

Lesson 22: Making An Appointment

In this lesson: *Making requests. Making an appointment. Morning, afternoon, evening. Before/after ___.*

Core Lesson

Dialogue

Foreigner A needs a haircut and hopes her Chinese acquaintance, Xiao Wang, will come along to provide assistance and moral support.

A: Xiǎo Wáng, nǐ xiàwǔ yǒu méiyǒu kòng? (Xiao Wang, you afternoon have free time?)

小王，你下午有没有空？

B：Shénme shì?（What business?）

什么事？

A：Bù hǎo yìsi máfán nǐ…（Embarrassed to trouble you…）

不好意思麻烦你……

A：…dànshì nǐ kěyǐ péi wǒ qù jiǎn tóufa ma?（...but you can accompany me go cut hair?）

……但是你可以陪我去剪头发吗？

A：Jiǎn tóufa yǐhòu，wǒ qǐng nǐ hē kāfēi.（Cut hair after，I invite you to drink coffee.）

剪头发以后，我请你喝咖啡。

B：Nǐ bú yòng zhème kèqi.（You not necessary so polite.）

你不用这么客气。

B：Wǒmen jǐdiǎn zài nǎli jiànmiàn?（We what time at where meet?）

我们几点在哪里见面？

A：Wǒmen sān diǎn zài lǐfàdiàn jiànmiàn，hǎo ma?（We 3:00 o'clock at barber shop meet，okay?）

我们三点在理发店见面，好吗？

B：Hǎo ba. Xiàwǔ jiàn.（Okay. Afternoon see.）

好吧。下午见。

Dialogue Vocabulary

xiàwǔ(afternoon)下午

shì(business, matter)事

bù hǎo yìsi(embarrassed)不好意思

péi(to accompany)陪

jiǎn(to cut)剪

tóufa(hair)头发

yǐhòu(after)以后

qǐng(to treat)请

zhème(so)这么

kèqi(polite)客气

jiànmiàn(to meet together)见面

lǐfàdiàn(barbershop)理发店

Additional Vocabulary

wèntí(question)问题

qǐng jiào (to respectfully ask)请教

yǐqián(before)以前

zuò(to do)做

zǎoshàng(morning)早上

wǎnshàng(evening)晚上

Useful Phrases

- Wǒ xiǎng wèn nǐ yī gè wèntí.

  (I want to ask you a question.)

- Wǒ xiǎng qǐng jiào yī gè wèntí.

  (I want to "request instruction" a question.)

This is a very polite way to introduce a question to an older person or someone of higher status.

- Wǒ xiǎng qǐng nǐ chī fàn.

  (I want to invite you to eat rice.)

  = I want to treat you to a meal.

- Xiàwǔ jiàn.

  (Afternoon see.)

  = See you this afternoon.

Also:

— Zǎoshàng jiàn. (Morning see.) = See you in the morning.

— Wǎnshàng jiàn. (Evening see.) = See you in the evening.

— Míngtiān jiàn. (Tomorrow see.) = See you tomorrow.

Sentence Patterns

How do I say " before/after (doing something)..."?

Pattern: (verb + noun) + yǐhòu/yǐqián.

Examples:

— Jiǎn tóufa yǐhòu… (Haircut after...) = After the haircut...

— Jiǎn tóufa yǐqián… (Haircut before...) = Before the haircut...

— Mǎi dōngxi yǐhǒu, wǒmen qù nǎli? (Buy things after, we go where?) = Where shall we go after we shop?

— Chī fàn yǐqián, wǒmen zuò shénme? (Eat before, we do what?) = What shall we do before we eat?

What is the sentence pattern for making an appointment (including time and place)?

Pattern: (subject) + (time) + (place) + (predicate).

Examples:

— Wǒmen sān diǎn zài lǐfàdiàn jiànmiàn ba. (We 3:00 at barbershop meet, okay?) = Let's meet at the barbershop at three.

— Nǐ míngtiān zài zhèr chī fàn ba. (You tomorrow at here eat, okay.) = Why don't you eat here tomorrow?

— Tā zǎoshàng zài huǒchē zhàn mǎi le huǒchē piào. (He morning at train station bought train ticket.) = He bought a train ticket at the train station (this) morning.

Notes

Strategy: Making Chinese friends.

Often you need to take some initiative in order to make Chinese friends, and one good strategy is to approach Chinese people for help or with questions about working and living in China. There is much, after all, that you need to learn, and your need for assistance plays to a deep-felt Chinese desire to be good hosts and help guests. Such an approach also puts you in a student role which "gives face" to whoever you ask for help. Sometimes little else grows out of such conversations, but sometimes they serve to break the ice and start a friendship.

Practice Ideas

Practice with a tutor

***Review*:**

Practice politely refusing a request.

***Tones / Pinyin / vocabulary*:**

Have your tutor dictate a number of short invitations to you (not necessarily from this lesson).

***Usage*:**

Practice making sentences using the (subject) + (time) + (place) + (predicate) pattern.

***Role play*:**

Practice making appointments.

Practice on the street

***RLP*:**

Approach a Chinese acquaintance with a request for help or an invitation.

Colloquial translation of Dialogue

A: Little Wang, do you have any free time this afternoon?

B: What's up?

A: I hate to bother you, but could you go with me to help me get a haircut? After the haircut I'll take you for a cup of coffee.

B: You don't need to be so polite. When should we meet and where?

A: How about meeting at 3:00 at the barber's?

B: Okay. See you this afternoon.

Lesson 23: Talking About Family

In this Lesson: *Inviting guests in. Family members. Conversation starters. Photos. Seeing guests off. Saying what someone does for a living. Signs: photo developing services.*

Core Lesson

Dialogue

Mary (A) answers a knock at the door and is pleasantly surprised to find Chinese colleague Teacher Wang (B).

A: Wáng lǎoshī! Qǐng jìn lái ba! (Wang Teacher!

Please enter!）

王老师！请进来吧！

B：Mǎlì, nǐ hǎo. Nǐ xiànzài máng ma?（Mary, how are you? You now busy?）

玛丽，你好。你现在忙吗？

A：Bù máng, bù máng. Jìn lái zuò.（Not busy, not busy. Enter come sit.）

不忙，不忙。进来坐。

……………

B：Zhè zhāng zhàopiān lǐ de rén shì shéi?（This picture in's is who?）

这张照片里的人是谁？

A：Zhè shì wǒ fùmǔ hé wǒ mèimei.（These are my parents and younger sister.）

这是我父母和我妹妹。

B：Nǐ de bàba zuò shénme gōngzuò?（Your father does what work?）

你的爸爸做什么工作？

A：Wǒ de bàba shì sījī.（My papa is driver.）

我的爸爸是司机。

B：Nǐ māma gōngzuò ma?（Your mother works?）

你妈妈工作吗？

B：Wǒ de māma zài yóujú gōngzuò.（My mother in

post office works.)

我的妈妈在邮局工作。

A：Nǐ de mèimei ne?（Your sister?）

你的妹妹呢?

B：Tā hái zài dú shū.(She still is studying.)

她还在读书。

B：Dànshì bìyè yǐhòu tā xiǎng zuò jǐngchá.(But graduate after she wants to be police.)

但是毕业以后她想做警察。

Dialogue Vocabulary

jìn(to enter)进

jìn lái(to come in)进来

zuò(to sit, to have a seat)坐

zhāng(*measure word for photos*)张

zhàopiān(photo)照片

lǐ(*suffix meaning* "*in*")里

fùmǔ(parents)父母

hé(and)和

mèimei(younger sister)妹妹

bàba(papa)爸爸

zuò(to work as)做

sījī(driver)司机

māma(mama)妈妈

dú shū(to study; to be a student)读书

bìyè(to graduate)毕业

jǐngchá(police)警察

Additional Vocabulary

jiā(home; family)家

lǎojiā(hometown)老家

zhàoxiàng (to take a photo)照相

xǐ (to wash; to develop film)洗

jiāojuǎn(photo film)胶卷

wán(to play)玩

***Family members*:**

fùqin(father)父亲

mǔqin(mother)母亲

gēge(older brother)哥哥

dìdi(younger brother)弟弟

jiějie(older sister)姐姐

xiōngdì(brother)兄弟

jiěmèi(sister)姐妹

érzi(son)儿子

nǚ'ér(daughter)女儿

háizi(child)孩子

Useful Phrases

***Common conversation starters*:**

- Nǐ jiā lǐ yǒu jǐ gè rén?

  (Your family has how many people?)

  = How many people are there in your family?

- Nǐ yǒu méiyǒu xiōngdì jiěmèi?

  (You have not have brothers sisters?)

  = Do you have any brothers or sisters?

- Nǐ yǒu háizi ma?

  (You have children?)

  = Do you have any children?

- Nǐ de lǎojiā zài nǎli?

  (Your hometown is where?)

  = Where is your hometown?

This is another very common opening conversation topic.

***Phrases related to photos*:**

- Nǐ xiǎng kàn zhàopiàn ma?

  (You want to see photos?)

- Wǒmen zhào (yī) gè xiàng ba.

  (Let's take a picture.)

- Wǒ xiǎng xǐ jiāojuǎn.

  (I want to develop film.)

***Phrases to say when guests depart*:**

- Màn zǒu.

  (Slowly walk.)

This is a fixed phrase that means something roughly like "Take care."

- Yǒu kòng lái zuò.

  (Have free time, come sit.)

  = When you have some time, come over and visit.

The phrases below are often used when seeing off a guest:

— Yǒu kòng lái wán. (Have free time, come play.)

— Yǒu kòng lái kàn wǒ. (Have free time, come see me.)

Sentence Patterns

How do you say something is in something else?

Pattern : (subject) + zài + (object) + lǐ(miàn).

Notice that lǐ or lǐmiàn *goes after the object*.

Examples:

— Miàn zài wǎn lǐmiàn. (Noodles at bowl inside.) =

The noodles are in the bowl.

— Nǐ de dìdi zài xuéxiào lǐ. (Your little brother at school in.) = Your little brother is in the school (building).

How do you say what someone does for a living?

There are three patterns in the Dialogue above.

Pattern #1: (who) + shì + (name of profession).

This is used to say someone "is a" teacher (student, etc.).

Examples:

— Wǒ de gēge shì yīshēng. (My older brother is doctor.) = My older brother is a doctor.

— Wǒ de jiějie shì hùshi. (My older sister is nurse.) = My older sister is a nurse.

Pattern #2: (who) + zài + (place) + gōngzuò.

This is used to say someone "works at/in" a school (hospital, etc.).

Examples:

— Wǒ de māma zài yīyuàn gōngzuò. (My mother at hospital works.) = My mother works at a hospital.

— Nǐ de bàba zài jiǔdiàn gōngzuò ma? (Your father at hotel works?) = Does your father work at a hotel?

Pattern #3: (who) + zuò + (name of profession).

This is used to say someone "works as a" doctor (nurse, etc.). This pattern is often used in sentences where "to work as" follows another verb or adjective.

Examples:

— Nǐ yuànyì zuò hùshi ma? (You willing to work as nurse?) = Are you willing to be a nurse?

— Nǐ xiǎng bù xiǎng zuò yīshēng? (You want to not want to be doctor?) = Do you want to become a doctor?

Notes

Lǎoshī:

Literally means "teacher" but sometimes used for other people as a term of respect. In the Dialogue above, "Teacher Wang" may actually be a teacher, but she may also just be an older educated person Mary is being respectful to.

Wán:

This word is used for adults' recreational activities as well as children's, so it is not exactly equivalent to the English word "play."

Dú shū:

Literally this means "read books." This means "to study" in two senses:

—#1: Tā hái zài dú shū. (He is still studying; i.e. still a student.)

—#2: Wǒmen jīn tiān wǎnshàng dú shū ba. (Let's study tonight.)

***Hosting guests*:**

A few tips on politely hosting Chinese guests to your home:

— Note how when Mary opens the door she addresses Teacher Wang, saying Wáng lǎoshī. Addressing someone by name and title in this manner when greeting them is considered polite and respectful in China.

— Teacher Wang politely asks if Mary is busy, and

Mary says she is not (whether she is in fact busy or not). Chinese hosts will almost never turn away a guest if possible, and will apologize profusely if it is necessary to turn away a guest, even an unexpected one.

— Chinese hosts will normally offer drinks and perhaps light snacks. You may need to offer several times before a guest will take refreshments (although not always), but you should keep trying. Often it is best to simply provide refreshments rather than asking if the guest wants any — the guest will virtually always say no whether he/she wants something or not.

Strategies: Social conversation.

Social conversation with new Chinese acquaintances often starts with questions about family members and what they do, and if you are in a Chinese home there is a very good chance this conversation will be conducted over a photo album. Having a photo album is also a good strategy when you have Chinese visitors and aren't quite sure what to talk about, especially if there is no common language you both speak comfortably. You might keep a photo album of your own handy as a tool to help you conduct simple Chinese conversations with visitors or other Chinese people you meet.

Practice Ideas

Practice with a tutor

***Review*:**

Practice making an appointment with your tutor.

***Tones / Pinyin / vocabulary*:**

Have your tutor dictate the names of some additional occupations to you. After the dictation, find out what they mean.

***Show and tell*:**

Bring in pictures of your family and talk with your tutor about them.

***Role play*:**

Role play hosting a guest in your home.

***Role play*:**

Role play buying film, getting film developed, and getting your camera fixed. Be sure to ask when to come back and pick up your developed film.

***Map reading*:**

Using the Survival Characters, see if you can locate a photo studio.

Practice on the street

***RLP*:**

Invite a Chinese friend to your apartment, and have a photo album ready.

***RLP*:**

Get film developed in a Chinese photo shop.

***Field trip*:**

Look for a place to get film developed.

Extra Credit

Survival Characters

The following may help you locate photo services:

照相馆　zhàoxiàngguǎn(photo studio)
冲洗胶卷　chōngxǐ jiāojuǎn(film developing)

Colloquial translation of Dialogue

A: Teacher Wang! Come in!

B: How are you, Mary. Are you busy now?

A: No, no. Come in and sit down.

……………………

B: Who are the people in this photo?

A: These are my parents and this is my younger sister.

B: What does your father do?

A: My father is a driver.

B: Does your mother work?

A: My mother works at a post office.

B: How about your younger sister?

A: She is still a student. But after she graduates she wants to join the police.

Lesson 24: Personal Questions

In this lesson: *Responding to personal questions foreigners often hear in China. Age. Marital status.*

Core Lesson

Dialogue

Foreigner B is in the middle of her first conversation with inquisitive but helpful Chinese neighbor A.

A: Nǐ chéng jiā le ma? (You have formed family?)
你成家了吗?

B: "Chéng jiā" shì shénme yìsi? ("Formed family" is

what meaning?)

成家是什么意思?

A: “Chéng jiā” shì “jiéhūn” de yìsi. (“Formed family” is “to marry's” meaning.)

成家是结婚的意思。

B: Ah, wǒ méiyǒu jiéhūn. (Oh, I haven't married.)

啊,我没有结婚。

A: Nàme, nǐ duó dà? (Well, you how old?)

那么,你多大?

B: Wǒ èrshí qī suì. (I twenty seven years old.)

我二十七岁。

A: Nǐ yīnggāi chéng jiā. (You should form family.)

你应该成家。

A: Wǒ gěi nǐ jièshào yī gè nán péngyou, hǎo ma? (I for you introduce a boyfriend, okay?)

我给你介绍一个男朋友,好吗?

B: Bú yòng, xièxie. (Not necessary, thanks.)

不用,谢谢。

B: Wǒ juéde dānshēn bú cuò. (I think single not bad.)

我觉得单身不错。

Dialogue Vocabulary

chéng jiā(to marry)成家
jiéhūn(to marry)结婚
suì(years old)岁
yīnggāi(should)应该
jièshào(to introduce)介绍
nán péngyou (boyfriend) 男朋友
juéde (to think that, to feel)觉得
dānshēn(single)单身
cuò(to make a mistake)错
bú cuò(not bad)不错

Additional Vocabulary

lǐmào(polite)礼貌
gōngzī(salary)工资
xiǎng(to miss)想
xíguàn (to be accustomed to)习惯
yǒu yìsi(to be interesting) 有意思
nǚ péngyou (girlfriend) 女朋友

Useful Phrases

***Other common personal questions*:**

- Nǐ yī gè yuè duōshao qián?

  (You one month how much money?)

= How much do you make a month?

This question is not uncommon in China.

Possible answers include:

— Wǒ yī gè yuè (amount) kuài qián.

(I one month ____ dollars.)

= I make ____ a month.

— Duìbuqǐ. Wàiguórén juéde zhè gè wèntí yǒu yīdiǎn bù lǐmào.

(Excuse me. Foreigners feel this question has a little not polite.)

- Nǐ de gōngzī duōshao qián?

(Your salary how much?)

= What is your salary?

Possible answers include:

— Wǒ yī nián (amount) kuài qián.

(I one year ____ dollars.)

= I make ____ a year.

— Wǒ de gōngzī bù gāo.

(My salary not high.)

- Nǐ xiǎng jiā ma?

(You miss home?)

Possible answers include:

— Wǒ hěn xiǎng jiā.

(I very miss home.)

= I miss home very much.

— Wǒ bù tài xiǎng jiā.

(I don't very miss home.)

= I don't miss home very much.

- Nǐ zài zhèli xíguàn ma?

(You here accustomed?)

= Are you accustomed to life here?

Possible answers include:

— Xíguàn.

(Accustomed.)

= Yes, I'm accustomed to it.

— Hái bú tài xíguàn.

(Still not very accustomed.)

- Nǐ juéde Zhōngguó zěnmeyàng?

(You think China how about?)

= What do you think about China?

Possible answers include:

— Wǒ hěn xǐhuān Zhōngguó.

(I very like China.)

— Wǒ juéde Zhōngguó hěn yǒu yìsi.

(I feel China very has meaning.)

= I feel China is very interesting.

Notes

Nǐ duō dà?

This way of saying "How old are you?" is more appropriate for adults than children. For children the question is: Nǐ jǐ suì?

Bú cuò:

This is used in ways similar to "Not bad!" in English.

Personal questions:

Many Chinese will be curious about you, and as you get into conversations you will be asked some questions which would be considered overly personal in Western countries. Of course it is up to you to decide how much or little to say in answer to these questions, but try not to take offense at them. Such questions are generally not ill-intended, and a rude response on your part may only confuse and offend a Chinese inquisitor who has no idea why you suddenly became so testy.

Practice Ideas

Practice with a tutor

***Review*:**

With pictures, review introducing your family.

***Tones/Pinyin/vocabulary*:**

Have your tutor think of a few other questions Chinese like to ask foreigners and dictate these to you. After the dictation, find out what they mean.

***Role play*:**

Decide how you want to respond to personal questions such as those above, and have your tutor teach you any necessary new expressions. Then have your tutor role play a nosey person as you practice responding.

Practice on the street

RLP:

You will probably have enough practice answering these questions even if you don't look for it. Good luck!

Colloquial translation of Dialogue

A: Have you formed a family?

B: What does "formed a family" mean?

A: "Formed a family" means to get married.

B: Oh, I'm not married.

A: Oh, how old are you?

B: I'm twenty-seven.

A: You should get married. How about if I introduce a boyfriend to you?

B: That's not necessary, thanks. I think being single is not bad.

Glossary

If you use the lessons in *Survival Chinese* out of order, you may often encounter unfamiliar vocabulary which is not explained in the lesson you are studying. In order to help you quickly discover the meanings of such words, below all of the vocabulary items from the Dialogue Vocabulary and Additional Vocabulary sections of each lesson are listed in alphabetical order.

bā(eight)八

ba(*suggestion particle*)吧

bàba(papa)爸爸

bái(white)白

bái cài(cabbage)白菜

báijiǔ(hard Chinese liquor)白酒

báiluóbo(turnip)白萝卜

bǎi(hundred)百

bǎihuò shāngdiàn(department store)百货商店

bàn(half)半

bāng(to help)帮

bāngmáng(to help)帮忙

bāo(a package of;a package)包

bǎo(full)饱

bāoguǒ(package)包裹

bāoguǒ dān(package notice)包裹单

bàoqiàn(apologetic)抱歉

bēi(a cup of)杯

bēizi(cup)杯子

bèi(back)背

Běijīng shì(Beijing city)北京市

běn(*measure word for books*)本

bízi(nose)鼻子

bǐ(compared to)比

bǐjiào(comparatively,rather)比较

bǐ(pen)笔

bìyè(to graduate)毕业

biǎo(meter)表

biéde(other)别的

bīngqílín(ice cream)冰淇淋

bīng shuǐ(ice water)冰水

bǐnggān(crackers,cookies)饼干

bìng(illness;to be sick)病

bówùguǎn(museum)博物馆

bózi(neck)脖子

bú cuò(not bad)不错

bú yòng(it's not necessary)不用

bù(not,no)不

bù hǎo yìsi(embarrassed)不好意思

cài (vegetable; generic term for meat/vegetable dishes)菜

càidān(menu)菜单

càihuā(cauliflower)菜花

cèsuǒ(toilet,bathroom)厕所

chá(tea)茶

chángtú(long distance)长途

chángtú chēzhàn(long distance bus station)长途车站

chāojí shìchǎng(supermarket)超级市场

chē(vehicle)车

chēzhàn(bus stop,bus station)车站

chēzi(vehicle)车子

chéng jiā(to marry)成家

chéngzi(orange)橙子

chī(to eat)吃

chōu yān(to smoke)抽烟

chuānghu(window)窗户

chūzūchē(taxi)出租车

cì(time, *as in "one time"*)次

cídiǎn(dictionary)词典

cōng(green onion)葱

cóng(from)从

cuò(wrong; to make a mistake)错

dǎ(to hit; to start a meter)打

dǎ diànhuà(make a phone call)打电话

dà(big)大

dà shēng(loud)大声

dàxué(university)大学

dài(to take, to bring)带

dānshēn(single)单身

dānwèi(work unit)单位

dànshì(but, however)但是

dào(to)到

de(*possessive marker*)的

děng(to wait)等

díshì(taxi)的士

dìdi(younger brother)弟弟

dìfang(place)地方

dìtú(map)地图

diǎn(o'clock)点

diànhuà(phone,phone call)电话

diànhuà hàomǎ(phone number)电话号码

diànnǎo(computer)电脑

diànzǐ yóujiàn(e-mail)电子邮件

dié(plate;a plate of)碟

dōngxi(thing)东西

dǒng(to understand)懂

dōu(both,all)都

dú shū(to study; to be a student)读书

dùzi(abdomen)肚子

duì(right,correct)对

duìbuqǐ(sorry;excuse me)对不起

duìhuànlǜ(exchange rate)兑换率

duìmiàn(opposite side)对面

duōjiǔ(how long)多久

duōshao(how much)多少

è(hungry)饿

érzi(son)儿子

ěrduo(ears)耳朵

èr(two,*ordinal—used in counting*)二

fā chuánzhēn(to send a fax)发传真

fàn(rice;food)饭

fāngbiàn(convenient)方便

fáng(room)房

fángjiān(a room)房间

fēijī chǎng(airport)飞机场

féizào(soap)肥皂

fēn(minute;minutes)分

fēnjī hàomǎ(extension number)分机号码

fēng(*measure word for letters*)封

fùmǔ(parents)父母

fùqin(father)父亲

gān(dry;to dry)干

gǎnmào(a cold;to have a cold)感冒

gāo(high,tall)高

gēge(older brother)哥哥

gè(*measure word*)个

gěi(to give)给

gōnggòng qìchē(public bus)公共汽车

gōngjīn(kilogram)公斤

gōngzī(salary)工资

gōngzuò(work,job;to work)工作

gōngzuòzhèng(work card)工作证

gòu(enough)够

guà hào(to register at hospital)挂号

guǎi wān(to turn a corner)拐弯

guì(expensive)贵

guójiā(country)国家

guàn(can,tin)罐

guàntou(can,tin)罐头

guǒzhī(fruit juice)果汁

hái(still,else)还

hái shì(or)还是

háizi(child)孩子

Hàn-Yīng(Chinese-English)汉英

Hànyǔ(Chinese language)汉语

hǎo(good)好

hàomǎ(number)号码

hē(to drink)喝

hé(and)和

hēi(black)黑

hěn(very)很

hóngsè(red)红色

hóulóng(throat)喉咙

hòumian(behind)后面

hòutiān(day after tomorrow)后天

húluóbo(carrot)胡萝卜

hùzhào(passport)护照

huài(bad;to break)坏

huàn(to exchange;to change)换

huáng(yellow)黄

huī(gray)灰

huì(can;able to)会

huǒchē(train;*lit*. fire vehicle)火车

huǒchē zhàn(train station)火车站

jī(chicken)鸡

jīhuì(opportunity)机会

jǐ(how many; several)几

jǐdiǎn(what time)几点

jì(to mail)寄

jiā(home;family)家

Jiānádà(Canada)加拿大

jiǎn(to cut)剪

jiànmiàn(to meet together)见面

jiǎng(to speak,to say)讲

jiāo(to teach)教

jiāohuàn(to exchange)交换

jiāojuǎn(photo film)胶卷

jiǎo(foot)脚

jiǎozi(pork/vegetable dumpling)饺子

jiào(to be called)叫

jiéhūn(to marry)结婚

jié zhàng(to count up a bill)结账

jiějie(older sister)姐姐

jiěmèi(sister)姐妹

jièshào(to introduce)介绍

jīn(catty)斤

jīntiān(today)今天

jìn(near)近

jìn(to enter)进

jìnbù(progress;to progress)进步

jìn lái(to come in)进来

jǐngchá(police)警察

jiǔ(nine)九

jiǔdiàn(hotel)酒店

juéde(to think that,to feel)觉得

kāfēi(coffee)咖啡

kǎchē(truck)卡车

kāi(to open)开

kāi shuǐ(boiled water)开水

kàn(to look,to read)看

kělè(cola)可乐

kěnéng(possible;possibly)可能

kěyǐ(may;permitted to)可以

kě(thirsty)渴

kèběn(textbook)课本

kèqi(polite)客气

kěndìng(definitely)肯定

kōngtiáo(air conditioner)空调

kòng(free time)空

kuài(Chinese dollar, *yuan*)块

kuài(fast)快

kuàizi(chopsticks)筷子

kuàngquánshuǐ(mineral water)矿泉水

lā dùzi(diarrhea;to have diarrhea)拉肚子

là(spicy hot)辣

lái(to come;to take)来

lán(blue)蓝

lǎojiā(hometown)老家

lǎoshī(teacher)老师

le(*perfective marker*)了

lěng(cold)冷

lí(Chinese pears)梨

lǐ(*suffix meaning* "*in*")里

lǐfàdiàn(barbershop)理发店

lǐmào(polite)礼貌

lǐmiàn(inside)里面

liànxí(to practice)练习

liǎng(1/10 catty)两

liǎng(two, *cardinal*)两

liù(six)六

lù(road)路

lǜ(green)绿

māma(mama)妈妈

máfan(trouble; to trouble)麻烦

mǎtǒng(toilet)马桶

ma(*question marker*)吗

mǎi(to buy)买

mài(to sell)卖

màn(slow)慢

máng(busy)忙

máojīn(towel)毛巾

mǎtou(dock)码头

méiyǒu(not have)没有

Měiguó(America)美国

mèimei(younger sister)妹妹

mén(door)门

mǐ fàn(cooked rice)米饭

miànbāo(bread)面包

miàn dí(small van taxi)面的

miàntiáo(noodles)面条

míngtiān(tomorrow)明天

míngzi(name,given name)名字

mótuōchē(motorcycle)摩托车

mǔqin(mother)母亲

ná(to get,to pick up,to carry)拿

nǎ(which)哪

nǎli(where)哪里

nà gè(that)那个

nàme(well,in that case...)那么

Nánjīng(Nanjing)南京

nán péngyou(boyfriend)男朋友

ne(*question marker*)呢

néng(able to)能

nǐ(you)你

nián(year)年

nín(*formal form for* "*you*")您

niúnǎi(milk)牛奶

nǚ'ér(daughter)女儿

nǚ péngyou(girlfriend)女朋友

nǚshì(Ms.)女士

pái duì(to stand in line)排队

péi(to accompany)陪

péngyou(friend)朋友

pífū(skin)皮肤

píjiǔ(beer)啤酒

piányi(inexpensive,cheap)便宜

piào(ticket)票

píng(*measure word* bottle)瓶

píngzi(bottle)瓶子

píngguǒ(apples)苹果

pútao jiǔ(wine)葡萄酒

qī(seven)七

qìchē(car;*lit*. steam vehicle)汽车

qìchē zhàn(bus station,bus stop)汽车站

qìshuǐ(soda pop)汽水

qiān(thousand)千

qiānbǐ(pencil)铅笔

qián(money)钱

qiánmian(ahead)前面

qiǎokèlì(chocolate)巧克力

qīngchu(clear;sure about)清楚

qīng cài(leafy green vegetable)青菜

qīngjiāo(green pepper)青椒

qǐng(please;to treat)请

qǐngjiào(to respectfully ask)请教

qù(to go)去

rè(hot)热

rén(person, people)人

Rìyǔ(Japanese language)日语

ròupiàn(pork slices)肉片

ruǎnjiàn(software)软件

sān(three)三

shàng(up; to get on)上

shàngwǎng(to go on-line)上网

shéi(who)谁

shénme(what)什么

shénmeyàng(what kind)什么样

shénmeyàng de(what kind of)什么样的

shí(ten)十

shíjiān(time)时间

shízài(really, truly)实在

shì(is)是

shì(business, matter)事

shǒu(hand, arm)手

shūcài(vegetables)蔬菜

shūdiàn(bookstore)书店

shūfu(comfortable)舒服

shǔ(to count)数

shuǐ(water)水

shuǐguǒ(fruit)水果

shuō(to say, speak)说

sījī(driver)司机

sì(four)四

suān(sour; sore)酸

suān là(sour-hot)酸辣

suì(years old)岁

tā(he, she, it)他,她,它

tāmen(they)他们,她们,它们

tài(too)太

tàitai(Mrs.; wife)太太

tāng(soup)汤

táozi(peaches)桃子

tiān(day)天

tián(sweet)甜

tīng(to listen)听

tíng(to stop)停

tòng(to hurt, to be painful)痛

tóu(head)头

tóufa(hair)头发

tǔdòu(potato)土豆

tuǐ(leg)腿

wàiguórén(foreigner)外国人

wàimian(outside)外面

wán(to play)玩

wǎn(bowl;a bowl of)碗

wǎnshàng(evening)晚上

wǎngbā(internet cafe)网吧

wǎngluò(the internet)网络

wàngjì(to forget)忘记

wèi(stomach)胃

wèi(hello)喂

wèijīng(MSG)味精

wèishēngzhǐ(toilet paper)卫生纸

wèn(to ask)问

wèntí(problem;question)问题

wǒ(I,me)我

wǔ(five)五

xīguā(watermelon)西瓜

xíguàn(to be accustomed to)习惯

xǐhuān(to like)喜欢

xǐ(to wash;to develop film)洗

xǐfàshuǐ(shampoo; *lit*. wash hair water)洗发水

xǐshǒujiān(washroom)洗手间

xiā(shrimp)虾

xià(down;to get off)下

xiàwǔ(afternoon)下午

xiānsheng(Mr.;husband)先生

xián(salty)咸

xiànzài(now)现在

xiāngjiāo(bananas)香蕉

xiǎng(want to;to miss)想

xiǎo(small)小

xiǎojiě(Miss;young woman)小姐

xiǎo bā(mini-van;*lit*. small bus)小巴

xiōngdì(brother)兄弟

xiōngkǒu(chest)胸口

xiě(to write)写

xièxie(thank you)谢谢

xìn(letter)信

xìnfēng(envelope)信封

xìnzhǐ(letter paper)信纸

xīnxiān(fresh)新鲜

xīngqītiān(Sunday)星期天

xíng(okay)行

xìng(surname)姓

xiūlǐ(to fix)修理

xué(to study)学

xuéshēng(student)学生

xuéxí(to study)学习

yáchǐ(tooth)牙齿

yágāo(toothpaste)牙膏

yánsè(color)颜色

yǎnjīng(eyes)眼睛

yángcōng(onion)洋葱

yǎng(itch; itchy)痒

yào(to want;will, need to)要

yào(medicine)药

yě(also)也

yī(one)一

yī bān lái shuō(in general, generally speaking)一般来说

yīdiǎn(a little)一点

yīxià(a moment)一下

yīfu(clothing)衣服

yīshēng(doctor)医生

yīyuàn(hospital)医院

yǐhòu(after)以后

yǐjīng(already)已经

yǐqián(before)以前

yìsi(meaning)意思

yínháng(bank)银行

yīnggāi(should)应该

Yīngguó(England)英国

Yīngyǔ(English)英语

yòng(to use)用

yóujú(post office)邮局

yóupiào(stamp)邮票

yǒu(have)有

yǒu yìsi(to be interesting)有意思

yòubian(right side)右边

yú(fish)鱼

yuǎn(far)远

yuànyì(to be willing)愿意

yuè(month;months)月

zài(again,also)再

zài(at, on, in, etc.)在

zàijiàn(goodbye)再见

zǎo(early;good morning)早

zǎoshàng(morning)早上

zěnme(how)怎么

zěnmele(what's wrong)怎么了

zěnmeyàng(how about)怎么样

zhāng(*measure word for maps, tickets, photos*)张

zhǎo(to look for; to visit)找

zhàopiān(photo)照片

zhàoxiàng(to take a photo)照相

zhè(this)这

zhème(so)这么

zhèr(here)这儿

zhīdao(to know)知道

zhǐ(paper)纸

zhōng(clock)钟

zhōng(middle)中

Zhōngguó(China)中国

zhǒng(kind, type)种

zhuǎn(to forward)转

zhuāng(to fill; to install)装

zhuāng ruǎnjiàn(to install software)装软件

zìjǐ(self; myself)自己

zìxíngchē(bicycle; *lit*. self-propelling vehicle)自行车

zǒu(to walk, to go, to leave)走

zǒu lù(to walk)走路

zuǐba(mouth)嘴巴

zuótiān(yesterday)昨天

zuǒbian(left side)左边

zuò(to do;to work as; to be)做

zuò(to sit;to take a vehicle)坐

Materials For Further Chinese Study

Chinese Study Materials:

***Chinese Language Learning For Foreigners* (Vol. 1 - 2). Wang Fuxiang et al. Sinolingua.**

Materials presented in both characters and *Pinyin*. Lessons are short and easy; but contain a limited amount of material. Good for someone who wants to review and consolidate elementary Chinese, adding somewhat to the material in *Survival Chinese*.

***Elementary Chinese Readers* (Vol. 1 - 4). Beijing Foreign Language Institute. Sinolingua. Revised edition. 1994.**

The dialogues and vocabulary lists have both characters and *Pinyin*, but the exercises are only presented in Chinese characters, so this set is best for students who want an introductory and intermediate course in written as well as spoken Chinese.

Chinese For Today **(Vol. 1 – 2). Beijing Foreign Language Institute. Commercial Press. 1986.**

Material nicely presented in both characters and *Pinyin*. Each book contains a considerable amount of material, so the series takes you well beyond where *Survival Chinese* leaves off. Tapes available. There is an additional book, *Exercises in Reading and Writing Chinese Characters*, to accompany Volume 1. Takes the learner well into the intermediate level. Good for someone who is looking for a solid beginning and intermediate program in both spoken and written Chinese.

Practical Chinese **(Vol. 1 – 3). Liu Yu, Liu Taihe, & Chen Tongsheng. Joint Publishing. 1995.**

Material nicely presented in both characters and *Pinyin*. More material than *Chinese for Today*, but lacks tapes. The set is relatively expensive, but takes the learner through the intermediate level and into fairly advanced material. Good for someone who is looking toward a sustained effort to learn Chinese.

A Course In Contemporary Chinese **(I－II). Li Dejin & Li Gengbin. Beijing Yuyan Xueyuan Chubanshe. 1988.**

This is actually two sets of 5 books, one set per level: Reading and Writing, Listening Exercise, Chinese Character Exercise, Listening, and Speaking. Tapes available. Needless to say, there is a lot of material. The Speaking and Listening books, along with the tapes, would provide a good oral skills course.

100 Putonghua Situations **:** ***Practical Chinese Conversation*** **. Peggy Wang. Commercial Press. 1995.**

Lots of bite-sized dialogues presented in characters, *Pinyin*, and English. Also includes vocabulary and notes. Tapes available.

I Can Read That **:** ***A Traveller's Introduction to Chinese Characters*** **. Julie Sussman. China Books and Periodicals. 1994.**

A fun introduction to Chinese characters, focusing on characters commonly seen on signs and elsewhere in daily Chinese life.

Books on language learning:

The Whole World Guide To Language Learning. **Terry Marshall. Intercultural Press. 1990.**

An introduction to how to carry out independent language study programs, working with mentors, for people who don't have access to formal language study programs.

Breaking The Language Barrier. **H. Douglas Brown. Intercultural Press. 1991.**

A general introduction to the factors involved in language learning. Takes a light, chatty approach. Primarily geared toward American high school and college students studying a foreign language in the US, but the general principles would apply to any language learning situation.

How To Be A More Successful Language Learner. 2nd ed. **Joan Rubin & Irene Thompson. Heinle and Heinle. 1994.**

A succinct general introduction to language learning.